B_

LIKE

JESUS

Am I Becoming the Person
God Wants Me to Be?

STUDY GUIDE | EIGHT SESSIONS

RANDY FRAZEE

ZONDERVAN™

ZONDERVAN

Be Like Jesus Study Guide
Copyright © 2020 by Randy Frazee

This title is also available as a Zondervan ebook.

Requests for information should be addressed to: Zondervan, 3900 Sparks Dr. SE, Grand Rapids, Michigan 49546

Portions of this guide were adapted from the *Believe Study Guide* (9780310826118) and from *Think, Act, Be Like Jesus* (9780310250173) by Randy Frazee.

ISBN 978-0-310-11838-1 (softcover)
ISBN 978-0-310-11839-8 (ebook)

First printing April 2020 / Printed in the United States of America

CONTENTS

HOW TO USE THIS GUIDE

Scope and Sequence

The goal of every follower of Jesus Christ is to become more like him, but how do you know where to start? What does it really mean to be a disciple of Jesus? The objective of *Be Like Jesus*—the third in a series of three small-group studies—is to continue the process of transforming your thoughts and actions so you can become like Jesus—the person whom God intended you to be. This study guide (and the related video) will help you assess your spiritual life, pinpoint areas that need special attention, and give you tools to help you grow. The first study in this series, *Think Like Jesus*, focused on the beliefs of the Christian faith. The next study, *Act Like Jesus*, focused on the practices of the Christian faith. This study will focus on the virtues of the Christian life. May God bless you as you seek him through this experience!

Session Outline

Each session is divided into two parts. In the group section, you and your group will begin by watching a short video teaching from Randy Frazee and follow along with the note-taking outline that has been provided. You will then recite the key verse, the key idea, and engage in some guided group discussion through the questions provided. At the end of the group time, you will be given real-life scenarios of people who struggle with their faith. Using the key applications from your study guide, your group will be challenged to think of ways to encourage the people within these case studies. Finally, you will close the group with a time of prayer.

Personal Study

At the end of the group section, you will find a series of readings and study questions for you to go through on your own during the week. Each of these sections will challenge you to consider a key question about the topic, think through a key idea, and then consider a key application regarding the difference it should make in your life. You will also be given four statements to help you evaluate the alignment of your life with the key idea and asked to take action by memorizing each session's key idea and key verse. **The personal study is a critical component in helping you see how the beliefs you are studying are reflected in the pages of the Bible, so be sure to complete this study during the week before your next group meeting.**

Group Size

Be Like Jesus is designed to be experienced in a group setting such as a Bible study, Sunday school class, or any small-group gathering. To ensure everyone has enough time to participate in discussions, it is recommended that large groups watch the video together and then break up into smaller groups of four to six people for discussion.

Materials Needed

Each participant should have his or her own study guide. Although the course can be fully experienced with just the video and study guide, participants are also encouraged to have a copy of *Believe: Living the Story of the Bible to Become Like Jesus*, which includes selections from the *New International Version* that relate to each week's session. Reading *Believe* as you go through the study will provide even deeper insights and make the journey even richer and more meaningful.

Facilitation

Each group should appoint a leader who is responsible for starting the video and for keeping track of time during discussions and activities. Leaders may also read questions aloud and monitor discussions, prompting participants to respond and ensuring that everyone has the opportunity to participate. (For more thorough instructions, see the Leader's Guide included at the back of this guide.)

Session 1

HOW DOES GOD WANT ME TO LOVE OTHERS?

WELCOME

Generations of poets and musicians have attempted to define and capture the essence of love throughout time. Yet the poems and songs just keep on coming. The reason? Love is such a powerful force that we never grow weary of hearing about it. Even still, we all struggle to adequately comprehend and express love to others on a daily basis. We know that God is the creator of all things—and therefore is the creator of love as well. So, we must look to him to understand what love truly means. He can reveal how we can hold his love in our hearts while giving it away at the same time—just as Jesus showed us throughout his life and in his death.

VIDEO TEACHING NOTES

Welcome to session one of *Be Like Jesus*. If this is your first time together as a group, take a moment to introduce your-selves to each other. As you watch the video, use the following outline to record some of the main points. (The answer key is found at the end of the session.)

- **Key Question**: What does it mean to sacrificially and unconditionally _____ _____ others?

- **Key Verse**: "This is love: not that we loved God, but that he loved us and sent his Son as an atoning sacrifice for our sins. Dear friends, since God so loved us, we also ought to love one another. No one has ever seen God; but if we love one another, God lives in us and his love is made _____ in us" (1 John 4:10–12).

- **Key Idea**: I am _____ to loving God and loving others.

- (**Key Application #1**): I am their _____ _____.

- (**Key Application #2**): I sacrifice my _____ to see them succeed.

- (**Key Application #3**): I help them see God's good _____ for them.

GETTING STARTED

Begin your discussion by reciting the key verse and key idea together as a group. On your first attempt, use your notes if you need help. On your second attempt, try to state them completely from memory.

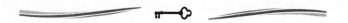

KEY VERSE: "This is love: not that we loved God, but that he loved us and sent his Son as an atoning sacrifice for our sins. Dear friends, since God so loved us, we also ought to love one another. No one has ever seen God; but if we love one another, God lives in us and his love is made complete in us" (1 John 4:10–12).

KEY IDEA: I am committed to loving God and loving others.

GROUP DISCUSSION

As a group, discuss your thoughts and feelings about the following declarations. Which statements are easy to declare with certainty? Which are more challenging? Why?

- God's grace enables me to forgive people who have hurt me.
- I rejoice when good things happen to other people.

- I demonstrate love equally toward people of all races.
- I frequently give up what I want for the sake of others.

Based on your group's dynamics and spiritual maturity, choose two or three questions that will lead to the best discussion about this week's key idea.

1. Who are the toughest people for you to love? Family members? Coworkers? Strangers? Explain why.

2. It's easy to love someone who meets your needs. But is it possible to genuinely love someone who does nothing for you or even hurts you? If so, how?

3. Outside of Jesus' example, when have you witnessed expressions of Christlike love?

Read Matthew 18:21–22, John 13:31–35, and 1 John 4:19–21, and then choose one or two questions that will lead to the greatest discussion in your group.

1. The Bible describes *love* as a quality that shows we belong to God. Given this, why do you think Christians are often described by outsiders as hypocritical and judgmental?

2. Based on what you read, what is the best strategy for developing authentic and genuine love for God and others?

3. *Forgiveness* is a key component of effectively loving one another. How can withholding forgiveness be an adversary of genuine love?

CASE STUDY

Use the following case study as a model for a real-life situation where you might put this week's key idea into practice.

> Bo's boss is not easy to work for. He shovels out criticism by the truckload, talks disrespectfully to his employees, and often takes credit for ideas that are not his own. Rumors have been circulating around the office that the boss's wife served him divorce papers over the weekend. He has basically locked himself in his office all week. When he does come out, he hardly says a word and looks awful.
>
> Most of the employees are reveling in their boss's pain, secretly making jokes and snarky comments. Bo has never liked the man, but something in his spirit won't allow him to join in with the other employees. He wonders if he should ask his boss if he's okay or just give him space. Does his boss deserve sympathy? Or is he simply reaping what he sowed?

Using the following key applications from this session, what could you say or do to help Bo exercise the virtue of love in this situation?

KEY APPLICATION #1: I am their advocate.

KEY APPLICATION #2: I sacrifice my rights to see them succeed.

KEY APPLICATION #3: I help them see God's good vision for them.

CLOSING PRAYER

Close your time together with prayer. Share your prayer requests with one another. Ask God to help you put this week's key idea into practice.

FOR NEXT WEEK

Before your next group meeting, be sure to read through the following personal study and complete the exercises.

VIDEO NOTES ANSWER KEY

love / complete /committed / advocate / rights / vision

PERSONAL STUDY

Every session in this guide contains a personal study to help you make meaningful connections between your life and what you are learning each week. Take some time after your group meeting each week to read through this section and complete the personal study. In total, the personal study should take about one hour to complete. Some people like to spread it out, devoting about ten to fifteen minutes a day. Others choose one larger block of time during the week to work through the entire personal study in one sitting. There is no right or wrong way to do this! Just choose a plan that best fits your needs and schedule from week to week, and then allow the Scripture to take root in your heart.

KEY QUESTION
WHAT DOES IT MEAN TO SACRIFICIALLY AND UNCONDITIONALLY LOVE OTHERS?

There is likely not a more abused word in the English language than *love*. We say we *love* chocolate, a song on the radio, and our favorite sports team just as we say we *love* our children. Are they the same? Of course not. But how does one differentiate the meaning? And what do we mean when we say we *love* God? Again, while those two concepts come from entirely different places in our hearts, we use the same word to describe our feelings for each.

The New Testament writers understood this dilemma. They wanted to talk about this new brand of Christian love that was made possible through a relationship with Jesus. Christ was good throughout his entire being. Goodness and love ruled his every motive, his every thought, his every word, and his every action. In and through his healings and miracles, he continually exhibited his goodness and love. Simply put, love dominates God's story.

But for the New Testament writers, there was no word in the Greek language that adequately described the nature and quality of this new divine experience of love. So, they took an existing word in the Greek language—*agape*—and infused it with new meaning to reflect this powerful concept of "God-centered love." The attempts of these human writers to describe God's love for us has resulted in a word that now has a meaning never before given.

> *This is love: not that we loved God, but that he loved us and sent his Son as an atoning sacrifice for our sins. Dear friends, since God so loved us, we also ought to love one another. No one has ever seen God; but if we love one another, God lives in us and his love is made complete in us* (1 John 4:10–12).

> *Love is patient, love is kind. It does not envy, it does not boast, it is not proud. It does not dishonor others, it is not self-seeking, it is not easily angered, it keeps no record of wrongs. Love does not delight in evil but rejoices with the truth. It always protects, always trusts, always hopes,*

always perseveres. Love never fails. . . . And now these three remain: faith, hope and love. But the greatest of these is love (1 Corinthians 13:4–8, 13).

Follow God's example, therefore, as dearly loved children and walk in the way of love, just as Christ loved us and gave himself up for us as a fragrant offering and sacrifice to God (Ephesians 5:1–2).

1. How would you define God-centered love as described in these passages?

_____

_____

_____

_____

2. How is forgiveness and sacrifice part of God's love?

_____

_____

_____

KEY IDEA
I AM COMMITTED TO LOVING GOD AND LOVING OTHERS

God asks us to love him with our heart, soul, and strength and then to love our neighbor as ourselves. This love has three distinct characteristics. First, *agape* love is unconditional. It is not dependent on love being given back. While it is always great for our feelings to be reciprocated, there are no conditions for God's love to be experienced. *Agape* love places no conditions, expectations, or stipulations on the other person for love to be expressed or displayed.

Second, *agape* love is sacrificial. It requires us to place the other person first and take a risk by showing your intent—regardless of the other person's response. This degree of love communicates, "I will lose some of who I am to love you. You are more important to me than I am to me!" *Agape* love gives itself up and takes risks for the welfare of others. As we exercise this type of love, we are reflecting the goodness of God in our motives and actions.

Third, *agape* love is forgiving. It expresses, "You don't have to be perfect for me to love you and stay in a relationship with you. In fact, I expect you to be imperfect, so I will forgive. You don't have to earn my love." This is what God does for us daily. He is a God who forgives us, and he invites us to do the same for others. Our commitment to God is thus reflected in our love for *him* and our extension of his love to others.

Jesus said, "A good man brings good things out of the good stored up in his heart" (Luke 6:45). As we seek to demonstrate *agape* love, we take steps to being more like Christ. And we find that when God's love is within us, loving others becomes quite possible.

> Hear, O Israel: The LORD our God, the LORD is one. Love the LORD your God with all your heart and with all your soul and with all your strength (Deuteronomy 6:4–5).

> Very rarely will anyone die for a righteous person, though for a good person someone might possibly dare to die. But God

demonstrates his own love for us in this: While we were still sinners, Christ died for us (Romans 5:7–9).

If we claim to be without sin, we deceive ourselves and the truth is not in us. If we confess our sins, he is faithful and just and will forgive us our sins and purify us from all unrighteousness (1 John 1:8–9).

1. What are the costs and benefits of loving God?

_____

_____

_____

_____

2. How does forgiveness help you to love others in your life unconditionally?

_____

_____

_____

_____

KEY APPLICATION
WHAT DIFFERENCE THIS MAKES

Jesus is our example. He received the love of the Father and passed it on to us. Our capacity to love thus begins with receiving God's love for us. When we yield to this presence in our lives, it enables us to love those whom we could never have loved before. It urges us to build others up instead of tear them down, to not pay back wrong for wrong, and to go the extra mile to do the hard things for others. It compels us to treat others with respect, regardless of how we are treated, and to love even those who seem unlovable.

Our world today has little time to spare for the homeless, the poor, the hungry, the orphaned, the diseased, the elderly, and the imprisoned. But Jesus clearly states that his followers are to be about his business in those very places—to show love to the unloved. This love of Jesus in our hearts enables us to show the world what true *agape* love looks like. Our love for him should be so strong and committed that all other loves can't possibly compare.

The amazing thing about God is that when we love him to this degree, our devotion and care for all people—including our families—grows in ever-increasing measure. We find we can't help but love everyone. This new breed of love allows us to be involved in healthy relationships and to be free to express God's love to the world. This love of others is confirmation that we are, in fact, children of God.

"My command is this: Love each other as I have loved you. Greater love has no one than this: to lay down one's life for one's friends" (John 15:12–13).

"You have heard that it was said, 'Love your neighbor and hate your enemy.' But I tell you, love your enemies and pray for those who persecute you, that you may be children of your Father in heaven" (Matthew 5:43–45).

We love because he first loved us (1 John 4:19).

1. How would you describe the love you show for others? How does this reflect your relationship with God?

_____

_____

_____

_____

2. What relationships has God given you through which you can share his love?

_____

_____

_____

_____

EVALUATE

As you conclude this personal study, use a scale of 1–6 to rate how strongly you believe the following statements (1 = no belief at all, 6 = complete confidence):

____ God's grace enables me to forgive people who have hurt me.

____ I rejoice when good things happen to other people.

____ I demonstrate love equally toward people of all races.

____ I frequently give up what I want for the sake of others.

TAKE ACTION

Memorizing Scripture is a valuable discipline for all believers to exercise. Spend a few minutes each day committing this week's key verse to memory.

KEY VERSE: "This is love: not that we loved God, but that he loved us and sent his Son as an atoning sacrifice for our sins. Dear friends, since God so loved us, we also ought to love one another. No one has ever seen God; but if we love one another, God lives in us and his love is made complete in us" (1 John 4:10–12).

Recite this week's key idea out loud. As you do, ask yourself, *Does my life reflect this statement?*

KEY IDEA: I am committed to loving God and loving others.

Answer the following questions to help you apply this week's key idea to your own life.

1. How could this virtue express itself in your life?

2. What visible attributes can be found in someone who embodies the virtues of love, kindness, and goodness?

_____

_____

_____

_____

_____

_____

3. What is impeding your ability to embrace this virtue? How can you overcome this obstacle?

_____

_____

_____

_____

_____

_____

4. What step can you take this week to love more like Jesus?

_____

_____

_____

_____

_____

_____

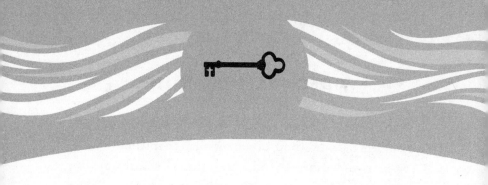

Session 2

WHAT WILL GIVE ME TRUE JOY?

Remember Eeyore and Tigger in the *Winnie the Pooh* books? For Eeyore, everything was doom and gloom, no matter what good circumstances came his way. For Tigger, everything was a carefree bounce through life, no matter what setbacks came his way. In our daily lives, it is easy to have the attitude of Eeyore while wishing we could have the outlook of Tigger—two extreme viewpoints of life. Yet the biblical brand of joy is not simply overcoming our inner Eeyore, nor is it strolling through life in ignorant bliss like our inner Tigger. Rather, biblical joy is to be found in facing each day's ups and downs through the contentment that Christ offers.

VIDEO TEACHING NOTES

Welcome to session two of *Be Like Jesus*. If there are any new members in your group, take a moment to introduce yourselves to each other. Spend a few minutes sharing any insights or questions about last week's personal study. Then start the video and use the following outline to record some of the main points. (The answer key is found at the end of the session.)

- **Key Question**: What gives us true happiness and _____ in life?

- **Key Verse**: "I have told you this so that my joy may be in you and that your joy may be _____ _____" (John 15:11).

- **Key Idea**: Despite my circumstances, I feel inner contentment and understand my _____ _____ in life.

- **(Key Application #1)**: Let your _____ _____ help you.

- **(Key Application #2)**: Saturate your _____ _____ with what the Bible has to say about joy.

- **(Key Application #3)**: _____ _____ and embrace God's intimate involvement and care in your life.

GETTING STARTED

Begin your discussion by reciting the key verse and key idea together as a group. On your first attempt, use your notes if you need help. On your second attempt, try to state them completely from memory.

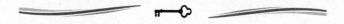

KEY VERSE: "I have told you this so that my joy may be in you and that your joy may be complete" (John 15:11).

KEY IDEA: Despite my circumstances, I feel inner contentment and understand my purpose in life.

GROUP DISCUSSION

As a group, discuss your thoughts and feelings about the following declarations. Which statements are easy to declare with certainty? Which are more challenging? Why?

- I have inner contentment even when things go wrong.
- Circumstances do not dictate my mood.
- I am excited about the sense of purpose I have for my life.
- I can be content with the money and possessions I now have.

Based on your group's dynamics and spiritual maturity, choose two or three questions that will lead to the best discussion about this week's key idea.

1. In what ways can you relate to Rozanne's story?

2. What are some practical ways to find joy in the midst of troubling times?

3. What biblical examples of joy inspire you (for example, the apostle Paul in prison)?

4. When have you witnessed joy? How have those demonstrations of joy motivated you to also remain joyful?

Read Psalm 16:1–11 and John 15:1–11 and choose one or two questions that will lead to the greatest discussion in your group.

1. Based on the passages you just read, what practical steps can you glean that will lead to greater joy in your life?

2. What are some unhealthy yet common beliefs and practices that stand in the way of true joy and contentment?

3. How does faith in Christ give you reason to be joyful in *all* circumstances?

CASE STUDY

Use the following case study as a model for a real-life situation where you might put this week's key idea into practice.

Haley joined your book club a few years back. As a group, you spend the first fifteen minutes checking in—asking about work, family, health, and hobbies. The discussion is uneventful until it is Haley's turn to speak. Her life seems to be a chaotic rollercoaster ride. It's either the best week of her life or it's a complete catastrophe. There is no in-between with her, and even when things are going well, she is anxious about the future. As her mentor, she has given you permission to speak honestly when you see areas for improvement in her life.

Using the following key applications from this session, what could you say or do to help Haley find joy in her life?

KEY APPLICATION #1: Let your community help you.

KEY APPLICATION #2: Saturate your mind with what the Bible has to say about joy.

KEY APPLICATION #3: Rehearse and embrace God's intimate involvement and care in your life.

CLOSING PRAYER

Close your time together with prayer. Share your prayer requests with one another. Ask God to help you put this week's key idea into practice.

FOR NEXT WEEK

Before your next group meeting, be sure to read through the following personal study and complete the exercises.

VIDEO NOTES ANSWER KEY

contentment / complete / purpose / community / mind / rehearse

PERSONAL STUDY

Last week, you examined the virtue of love. Perhaps you were challenged to unconditionally love and show kindness and goodness to even the most challenging people in your life. Before your next group meeting, complete the following study. Take some time to allow the Scripture to enter your mind and to evaluate what truly brings you joy in life.

KEY QUESTION

WHAT GIVES US TRUE HAPPINESS AND CONTENTMENT IN LIFE?

The first order of business is to identify the difference between joy and happiness. For many people today, being happy is dependent on whether life is "all good." They rate their happiness on how they perceive negative issues going on at the time. When problems arise, their happiness goes south. When troubles begin to go away, the happy scale starts to climb.

However, real joy is not dependent on circumstances. Ironically, it becomes the strongest when trouble comes. We can have all the possessions, health, and good looks we desire . . . but life will still prove to be challenging if we don't have joy. The good news is that Christ offers us this joy—and it is a joy that lasts no matter what we face. This is because it is rooted in the key belief that the one true God is a personal God who is involved in and cares about our daily lives. He loves us and is working out a good plan for us. When we confidently believe this in our hearts, we can rise above our circumstances and find joy in Christ alone.

God may shower us with blessings and circumstances that bring joy to our lives, but true joy is found not in those things themselves—only in their source.

"The joy of the LORD is your strength" (Nehemiah 8:10).

Let all who take refuge in you be glad;
let them ever sing for joy (Psalm 5:11).

You make known to me the path of life;
you will fill me with joy in your presence,
with eternal pleasures at your right hand
(Psalm 16:11).

"As the Father has loved me, so have I loved you. Now remain in my love. If you keep my commands, you will remain in my love, just as I have kept my Father's commands and remain in his love. I have told you this so that my joy may be in you and that your joy may be complete" (John 15:9–11).

1. How would you describe the relationship between true happiness and contentment?

_____

_____

_____

_____

_____

2. Why is it sometimes difficult for people who have plenty to be content?

_____

_____

_____

_____

KEY IDEA

DESPITE MY CIRCUMSTANCES, I FEEL INNER CONTENTMENT AND UNDERSTAND MY PURPOSE IN LIFE

Joy has more to do with remaining in God's presence than with avoiding struggles in our lives. Joy is always available to us when we remain in Christ. The apostle Paul learned this secret to joy and was able to confidently state that he could be content "whatever the circumstances" (Philippians 4:11). James discovered that joy had nothing to do with eliminating negative circumstances but with embracing them as positive opportunities to strengthen faith—which "produces perseverance" (James 1:3).

Thus, we find that not only can we have joy in spite of our difficult circumstances, but also our joy can actually *grow* through our difficult circumstances. Yet this kind of joy is only available in Jesus. Furthermore, when we come alongside Jesus by sharing in his work, serving others out of love, and working to bring people to him, we become a part of the celebration that is going on in heaven right here and right now (see Luke 15:3–7).

Celebrating God's involvement in our lives evokes joy. Only Jesus can make our lives flourish in the midst of trouble because in him joy is strengthened—often even when life is challenging. When we focus on what God has done for us through Christ in the past, and rest on his promises for the future, we can have joy in the present.

I have learned to be content whatever the circumstances. I know what it is to be in need, and I know what it is to have plenty. I have learned the secret of being content in any and every situation, whether well fed or hungry, whether living in plenty or in want. I can do all this through him who gives me strength (Philippians 4:11–13).

Consider it pure joy, my brothers and sisters, whenever you face trials of many kinds, because you know that the testing of your faith produces perseverance. Let perseverance finish its work so that you may be mature and complete, not lacking anything (James 1:2–4).

I thank my God every time I remember you. In all my prayers for all of you, I always pray with joy because of your partnership in the gospel from the first day until now, being confident of this, that he who began a good work in you will carry it on to completion until the day of Christ Jesus (Philippians 1:3–5).

1. How can opportunities to share Jesus with others bring joy into your life?

   _____

   _____

   _____

   _____

2. What role does your attitudes play in being able to experience joy?

_____

_____

_____

_____

KEY APPLICATION
WHAT DIFFERENCE THIS MAKES

When we walk in biblical joy, it becomes the filter through which we see life. We're not talking about putting on rose-colored glasses but about actually having brand-new eyes! Having joy is not a matter of sticking our head in the sand and bouncing through life (like Tigger) but rising above our circumstances by adopting an eternal mindset. We can put aside worry, fret, and fear because we recognize that even though we may not be in control, God is *always* in control. He is in charge of the outcome, and joy comes from trusting the controller of all things.

Joy lifts others up. If we choose to practice joy on a regular basis, we will not only be far more approachable and relatable people, but also our attitude will rub off on others and make a big impact on all the environments in which we find ourselves. When those around us can see that we *choose* to express joy in spite of our circumstances, our lives become a powerful testimony for Christ. As we experience the inward transformation of our thoughts, it becomes an outward expression in our actions that attracts people to Christ.

We all will have good and bad days. We will all experience life's ups and downs. But this doesn't have to rob us of our joy. Happiness is all too fleeting, but the joy of Jesus is available to our soul right now. When trials arise, we can choose to lean on him . . . and we will find his joy.

> *Though the fig tree does not bud*
> *   and there are no grapes on the vines,*
> *though the olive crop fails*
> *   and the fields produce no food,*
> *though there are no sheep in the pen*
> *   and no cattle in the stalls,*
> *yet I will rejoice in the Lord,*
> *   I will be joyful in God my Savior*
> (Habakkuk 3:17–18).

> *Do everything without grumbling or arguing, so that you may become blameless and pure, "children of God without fault in a warped and crooked generation." Then you will shine among them like stars in the sky as you hold firmly to the word of life* (Philippians 2:14–16).

> *Rejoice in the Lord always. I will say it again: Rejoice! Let your gentleness be evident to all. The Lord is near* (Philippians 4:4–5).

1. How can joy change your perspective and perception of negative circumstances?

2. How has growing in God's joy been a part of your life as a believer in Christ?

_____

_____

_____

_____

_____

_____

EVALUATE

As you conclude this personal study, use a scale of 1–6 to rate how strongly you believe the following statements (1 = no belief at all, 6 = complete confidence):

_____ I have inner contentment even when things go wrong.

_____ Circumstances do not dictate my mood.

_____ I am excited about the sense of purpose I have for my life.

_____ I can be content with the money and possessions I now have.

TAKE ACTION

Memorizing Scripture is a valuable discipline for all believers to exercise. Spend a few minutes each day committing this week's key verse to memory.

KEY VERSE: "I have told you this so that my joy may be in you and that your joy may be complete" (John 15:11).

Recite this week's key idea out loud. As you do, ask yourself, *Does my life reflect this statement?*

KEY IDEA: Despite my circumstances, I feel inner contentment and understand my purpose in life.

Answer the following questions to help you apply this week's key idea to your own life.

1. How would this virtue express itself in your life?

2. What visible attributes can be found in someone who manifests the virtue of joy?

3. What is impeding your ability to choose a lifestyle of joy? How can you overcome this obstacle?

_____
_____
_____
_____
_____
_____

4. What step can you take this week to increase the presence of joy in your daily life?

_____
_____
_____
_____
_____
_____

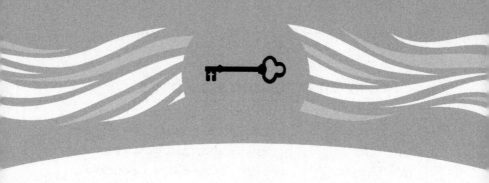

Session 3

HOW DO I FIND REAL PEACE?

WELCOME

Most people would define peace as a feeling—as a sensation in the soul. We want to trade our anxiety, depression, and fear for tranquility, and we often adopt harmful and temporal practices to achieve this feeling. Substances such as drugs and alcohol can create an artificial "peace" and sedate our mood. The problem comes when the feeling wears off and we are left, once again, with the chaos of our soul. Biblical peace is not based on feelings or circumstances. In the Bible, the presence of peace is about right relationships with God and our neighbors. We can find the strength to battle anxiety in right relationships—with God, others, and ourselves.

VIDEO TEACHING NOTES

Welcome to session three of *Be Like Jesus*. Spend a few minutes sharing any insights or questions about last week's personal study. Then start the video and use the following outline to record some of the main points. (The answer key is found at the end of the session.)

- **Key Question**: Where do I find _____
  _____ to battle anxiety and fear?

- **Key Idea**: I am free from _____
  because I have found peace with God, peace with others, and peace with myself.

- **Key Verse**: "Do not be anxious about anything, but in every situation, by prayer and petition, with
  _____,
  present your requests to God. And the peace of God, which transcends all understanding, will guard your hearts and your minds in Christ Jesus" (Philippians 4:6–7).

- **(Key Application #1)**: Come to _____
  _____ in your relationship with God.

- **(Key Application #2)**: As much as it is up to you, live at peace with all _____.

- **(Key Application #3)**: Learn to live at peace with
  _____.

GETTING STARTED

Begin your discussion by reciting the key verse and key idea together as a group. On your first attempt, use your notes if you need help. On your second attempt, try to state them completely from memory.

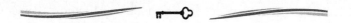

KEY VERSE: "Do not be anxious about anything, but in every situation, by prayer and petition, with thanksgiving, present your requests to God. And the peace of God, which transcends all understanding, will guard your hearts and your minds in Christ Jesus" (Philippians 4:6–7).

KEY IDEA: I am free from anxiety because I have found peace with God, peace with others, and peace with myself.

GROUP DISCUSSION

As a group, discuss your thoughts and feelings about the following declarations. Which statements are easy to declare with certainty? Which are more challenging? Why?

- I know God has forgiven me because of what Jesus has done.
- I am not angry with God, myself, or others.

- I forgive people who deeply hurt me.
- I have an inner peace from God.

Based on your group's dynamics and spiritual maturity, choose two or three questions that will lead to the best discussion about this week's key idea.

1. Although true peace is accessible to all who call Jesus Christ their "Lord," many continue to live with fear and anxiety. Why do you think this is the case?

2. What are some biblical ways to overcome fear and anxiety? What have you found to be most successful?

3. Who in your life maintains a state of peace even in the most troubling situations? What part does faith play in that person's ability to remain at peace?

4. What thoughts or behaviors tend to feed your feelings of fear and anxiety? What boundaries can you set in place to avoid those pitfalls?

_____

_____

_____

_____

_____

CASE STUDY

Use the following case study as a model for a real-life situation where you might put this week's key idea into practice.

> Your neighbor Kyle has been coming to church with you for about a year. He was baptized this summer and is trying to read the Bible on his own. He calls you occasionally when he runs into passages that he doesn't understand. During a recent conversation, Kyle admitted, "I'm grateful for what God has done in my life. I want to make it up to him, but I've done way too many rotten things. I'm afraid I'll never be able to make things right with him. Honestly, I spend most nights tossing and turning, wondering how I can undo the mistakes from my past."

Using the following key applications from this session, discuss what you could say or do to help Kyle make peace with his past.

KEY APPLICATION #1: Come to peace in your relationship with God.

KEY APPLICATION #2: As much as it is up to you, live at peace with all people.

KEY APPLICATION #3: Learn to live at peace with yourself.

CLOSING PRAYER

Close your time together with prayer. Share your prayer requests with one another. Ask God to help you put this week's key idea into practice.

FOR NEXT WEEK

Before your next group meeting, be sure to read through the following personal study and complete the exercises.

VIDEO NOTES ANSWER KEY
strength / anxiety / thanksgiving / peace / people / yourself

PERSONAL STUDY

Last week you examined the virtue of joy. Perhaps you learned that God is the only true source of authentic joy. Before your next group meeting, complete the following study. Allow the Scripture to enter your mind and release any anxiety that you may be feeling.

KEY QUESTION
WHERE DO I FIND STRENGTH TO BATTLE ANXIETY AND FEAR?

If you were to ask people to give you a definition of peace, you would likely hear more about the absence of trouble than the presence of contentment. A biblical definition of peace refers not to the *subtraction* of anything but to the *addition* of Jesus. In the Bible, we read about winning favor in the sight of God and people (see Proverbs 3:4) or growing in favor with God and people (see 1 Samuel 2:26; Luke 2:52). This indicates a peace with God (vertical) and a peace with others (horizontal). Relationships are complete, respect is intact, and we have peace. Wherever Christ is present, peace is available.

Jesus Christ is the Prince of Peace (see Isaiah 9:6), not only in the future kingdom of heaven but in our lives as well. The pouring out of his lifeblood produced the possibility of a life of peace between us and God. Because this peace of God is available to everyone, the barriers that once separated people have come crashing down. Through the saving work of Jesus' death and resurrection, all believers share citizenship in God's kingdom of peace.

So, if we want greater peace in our lives, we should first seek to live in obedience to God and then apply his wisdom to find peace in our relationships with others.

Do not be anxious about anything, but in every situation, by prayer and petition, with thanksgiving, present your requests to God. And the peace of God, which transcends all understanding, will guard your hearts and your minds in Christ Jesus (Philippians 4:6–7).

Therefore, since we have been justified through faith, we have peace with God through our Lord Jesus Christ, through whom we have gained access by faith into this grace in which we now stand (Romans 5:1–2).

For he himself is our peace, who has made the two groups one and has destroyed the barrier, the dividing wall of hostility, by setting aside in his flesh the law with its commands and regulations. His purpose was to create in himself one new humanity out of the two, thus making peace, and in one body to reconcile both of them to God through the cross, by which he put to death their hostility (Ephesians 2:14–16).

1. How does Jesus establish peace between you and God and between you and others?

_____

_____

_____

2. What do you think are the primary reasons that people experience fear and anxiety? How can God's presence change this situation?

_____

_____

_____

_____

KEY IDEA

I AM FREE FROM ANXIETY BECAUSE I HAVE FOUND PEACE WITH GOD, PEACE WITH OTHERS, AND PEACE WITH MYSELF

Worry is the chief robber of peace. Perhaps this is why we often find Jesus, the Prince of Peace, emphasizing the fact that God loves and cares for his people individually and doesn't want the worries of this life to overtake them. Jesus provided the opportunity for people to have peace with God. His death on the cross satisfied God's wrath against our sin. Yet we must choose to receive this peace that is only offered through salvation . . . and then live it out.

In our relationships, we must practice peace whenever it is possible—whenever we have the ability to facilitate peace. Of course, living at peace with others, even with our fellow believers, can be a challenge. After all, we each think, feel, and react differently. We are all sinners, so peace will evade us at times. Furthermore, peace won't always be everyone else's choice. Yet we are still called to do all we can to live in peace. Even when others won't allow it, we can be at peace with ourselves and be ready to offer peace to others.

Jesus' peace is *always* available to us. Even when it comes to those we would consider our enemies, our God can work miracles. Peace is a choice that comes out of our relationship with God. The Lord is present even in the noise of the world and in the face of those who hate us, so peace is always present. We are to set our sights on living at peace with everyone.

> *Peace I leave with you; my peace I give you. I do not give to you as the world gives. Do not let your hearts be troubled and do not be afraid* (John 14:27).

> *Do not repay anyone evil for evil. Be careful to do what is right in the eyes of everyone. If it is possible, as far as it depends on you, live at peace with everyone* (Romans 12:17–18).

> *Let us therefore make every effort to do what leads to peace and to mutual edification* (Romans 14:19).

> *In peace I will lie down and sleep,*
>   *for you alone, LORD,*
>   *make me dwell in safety* (Psalm 4:8).

1. How does viewing peace as a choice rather than a feeling or state of mind influence the way you respond to tension in relationships?

_____

_____

_____

_____

_____

2. How can peace with God change the hold that fear and anxiety have in your life?

_____

_____

_____

_____

KEY APPLICATION
WHAT DIFFERENCE THIS MAKES

When Christians are asked about their lives prior to salvation, we hear a consistent testimony that they were searching for internal peace because they hadn't had it in their lives. We also hear people say after praying to receive Christ, "I just immediately felt a peace come over me." While this is a feeling, it is also the spiritual sensation of God depositing his peace into our souls. This is no flippant, figurative statement, but a literal change of the heart. The presence of peace comes to live forever in a warring soul.

We must remember that a nonbeliever cannot muster up God's peace. For this reason, a discussion about peace can open a doorway to reaching those who do not know Christ. After all, who doesn't want to have peace? Every human throughout history has sought it. Regardless of what we may attempt to stuff into our souls, nothing will satisfy or accomplish what Christ can do. His brand of peace is the only one that is custom-built to fit our hearts.

If Jesus is the answer, then we have the answer. If he is the Prince of Peace, we now hold him in our hearts. This allows us to speak peace into volatile situations, promote peace in the midst of madness, and carry peace into confusion. We should never gain the reputation for divisiveness and dysfunction but live in such a way that we are known for harmony and unity. This atmosphere is found in the mindset of Christ, and as his temples moving about in the world, we can be known as purveyors of peace.

When it comes to difficult situations we can't immediately fix, we must go first to God in prayer. We can offer to him the things beyond our control. As we engage in this spiritual practice of prayer, a peace beyond our comprehension begins to grow in our hearts. And when this peace becomes the foundation of our souls, the walls of our lives will be stable. God's peace will steady and maintain our thoughts, emotions, attitudes, and feelings. As we surrender daily to Christ when the storms of life threaten, his peace will keep us grounded and secure.

> *"The LORD bless you*
> *and keep you;*
> *the LORD make his face shine on you*
> *and be gracious to you;*
> *the LORD turn his face toward you*
> *and give you peace"* (Numbers 6:24–26).

Let the peace of Christ rule in your hearts, since as members of one body you were called to peace (Colossians 3:15).

But seek first his kingdom and his righteousness, and all these things will be given to you as well. Therefore do not worry about tomorrow, for tomorrow will worry about itself. Each day has enough trouble of its own (Matthew 6:33–34).

1. How is God's peace evident in your life? What makes this appealing to non-believers?

_____

_____

_____

_____

_____

2. When worry or disagreements arise, what can you do to respond to the situation and bring peace?

_____

_____

_____

_____

_____

EVALUATE

As you conclude this personal study, use a scale of 1–6 to rate how strongly you believe the following statements (1 = no belief at all, 6 = complete confidence):

_____ I know God has forgiven me because of what Jesus has done.

_____ I am not angry with God, myself, or others.

_____ I forgive people who deeply hurt me.

_____ I have an inner peace from God.

TAKE ACTION

Memorizing Scripture is a valuable discipline for all believers to exercise. Spend a few minutes each day committing this week's key verse to memory.

KEY VERSE: "Do not be anxious about anything, but in every situation, by prayer and petition, with thanksgiving, present your requests to God. And the peace of God, which transcends all understanding, will guard your hearts and your minds in Christ Jesus" (Philippians 4:6–7).

Recite this week's key idea out loud. As you do, ask yourself, *Does my life reflect this statement?*

KEY IDEA: I am free from anxiety because I have found peace with God, peace with others, and peace with myself.

Answer the following questions to help you apply this week's key idea to your own life.

1. How would this virtue express itself in your life?

_____

_____

_____

2. What visible attributes can be found in someone who lives at peace?

_____

_____

_____

_____

_____

3. What is impeding your ability to experience true peace? How can you overcome this obstacle?

_____

_____

_____

_____

_____

4. What step can you take this week to experience greater peace with God, with others, and with yourself?

_____

_____

_____

_____

_____

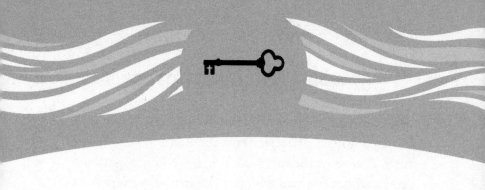

Session 4

HOW DOES GOD FREE ME FROM SINFUL HABITS?

---------- **WELCOME** ----------

The Bible refers to our bodies, as well as the sin we create by our choices, as the "flesh." Our flesh wants to take care of itself and always be first, no matter the cost to anyone—including, ironically, our own selves. The flesh causes damage, even to the point of self-destruction. In this state, we are separated from God—essentially having no choice but to opt for self. While we can make good choices and do good deeds, we cannot keep our behavior consistent, simply because of our fleshly nature. But the grace we receive after salvation gives us a new choice. We can now choose either to go our own way or God's way. We can say *no* anytime we choose by obeying God. Through Christ, we can practice self-control rather than be out-of-control.

VIDEO TEACHING NOTES

Welcome to session four of *Be Like Jesus*. Spend a few minutes sharing any insights or questions about last week's personal study. Then start the video and use the following outline to record some of the main points. (The answer key is found at the end of the session.)

- **Key Question:** How does God _____ me from addictions and sinful habits?

- **Key Verse:** "For the grace of God has appeared that offers salvation to all people. It teaches us to say 'No' to ungodliness and worldly passions, and to live _____, upright and godly lives in this present age, while we wait for the blessed hope—the appearing of the glory of our great God and Savior, Jesus Christ" (Titus 2:11–13).

- **Key Idea:** I have the power through _____ _____ to control myself.

- **(Key Application #1):** Self-control is _____ _____ by the grace of God, not the law.

- **(Key Application #2):** Self-control is empowered through _____ - _____.

- **(Key Application #3):** Self-control is helped along through loving _____.

GETTING STARTED

Begin your discussion by reciting the key verse and key idea together as a group. On your first attempt, use your notes if you need help. On your second attempt, try to state them completely from memory.

KEY VERSE: "For the grace of God has appeared that offers salvation to all people. It teaches us to say 'No' to ungodliness and worldly passions, and to live self-controlled, upright and godly lives in this present age, while we wait for the blessed hope—the appearing of the glory of our great God and Savior, Jesus Christ" (Titus 2:11–13).

KEY IDEA: I have the power through Christ to control myself.

GROUP DISCUSSION

As a group, discuss your thoughts and feelings about the following declarations. Which statements are easy to declare with certainty? Which are more challenging? Why?

- I am not addicted to any substances—whether food, caffeine, tobacco, alcohol, or chemicals.
- I do not burst out in anger toward others.

- I do not have sexual relationships that are contrary to biblical teaching.
- I control my tongue.

Based on your group's dynamics and spiritual maturity, choose two or three questions that will lead to the best discussion about this week's key idea.

1. When is it most difficult to maintain self-control?

2. Who is someone who amazes you with his or her ability to maintain self-control?

3. Christians often "try harder" to resist sin, but ultimately fail. What is a better way to combat our sinful urges?

4. What role can biblical community play in building self-control in your life?

_____

_____

_____

_____

Read Titus 2:1–15 and choose one or two questions that will lead to the greatest discussion in your group.

1. In what way is grace a more effective motivator to resist sin than fear? Can you think of some real-life examples?

_____

_____

_____

_____

2. What worldly passions do you have a hard time saying no to?

_____

_____

_____

_____

3. How can focusing on the return of Christ expand your ability to be self-controlled?

_____

_____

_____

_____

CASE STUDY

Use the following case study as a model for a real-life situation where you might put this week's key idea into practice.

> Molly is one of those people who seems to know everyone. A social butterfly, she is the life of the party wherever she goes. You really enjoy spending time with her, but there are always moments with her that make you feel uncomfortable. Because of her vast array of friends, she knows the juiciest gossip and loves to share it. Although you know it is wrong, you can't help but get sucked into the conversation. Before you know it, you are openly discussing your coworkers' and friends' darkest moments.

Using the following key applications from this session, discuss what you could do to avoid making this mistake again.

KEY APPLICATION #1: Self-control is motivated by the grace of God, not the law.

KEY APPLICATION #2: Self-control is empowered through God-control.

KEY APPLICATION #3: Self-control is helped along through loving accountability.

CLOSING PRAYER

Close your time together with prayer. Share your prayer requests with one another. Ask God to help you put this week's key idea into practice.

FOR NEXT WEEK

Before your next group meeting, be sure to read through the following personal study and complete the exercises.

VIDEO NOTES ANSWER KEY
free / Christ / self-controlled / motivated /
God-control / accountability

PERSONAL STUDY

Last week you examined the virtue of peace. Maybe you were personally challenged to live at peace in a particular area of struggle—with God, with others, or with yourself. Before your next group meeting, complete the following study. Allow the Scripture to enter your mind as you evaluate your ability to be self-controlled.

KEY QUESTION
HOW DOES GOD FREE ME FROM ADDICTIONS AND SINFUL HABITS?

As we talk about self-control, we think of taming and over-throwing the flesh. Everyone at some point struggles with self-control—it's the presence of the sin nature within us. Essentially, there is a constant internal attack going on within us at all times. Temptation, thoughts, and attitudes flow through us, wanting self to be on the throne and get its own way.

The world is an external destructive influence that attacks us as well. The Bible defines the *world* as the lust from our hearts brought on from us wanting all we see—with pride as the ultimate root driving this systemic problem. Perhaps this is why we find a big fat *I* smack in the middle of the word *pride*! Whether the motivation to place ourselves first comes from an internal motivation or an external one, the flow of communication is the flesh telling our heart what to do. The flesh is bossing, sometimes even bullying, the heart around.

God desires us to demonstrate self-control. However, in the face of all of these pressures, the battle to keep our sinful nature in check can be easier said than done. How do we counter this constant attack? We choose God over self.

> Like a city whose walls are broken through
>   is a person who lacks self-control (Proverbs 25:28).

> For what the law was powerless to do because it was weakened by the flesh, God did by sending his own Son in the likeness of sinful flesh to be a sin offering. And so he condemned sin in the flesh, in order that the righteous requirement of the law might be fully met in us, who do not live according to the flesh but according to the Spirit (Romans 8:3–4).

> For the grace of God has appeared that offers salvation to all people. It teaches us to say "No" to ungodliness and worldly passions, and to live self-controlled, upright and godly lives in this present age (Titus 2:11–12).

1. What forces tend to keep you from having self-control?

_____

_____

_____

2. How is God's presence in your life a key to growing in self-control?

_____

_____

_____

KEY IDEA
I HAVE THE POWER THROUGH CHRIST TO CONTROL MYSELF

Self-control might be better understood as *God*-control. We control ourselves by giving control over to God. We surrender, the flesh gives up, and God takes command. In fact, self-control is best achieved when harnessed to the practice of total surrender. After all, how can anyone make strong headway at self-control without first surrendering to God's Spirit? How can someone totally surrender to God without developing self-control?

The two work independently, yet together—each supporting and strengthening the other. As we *yield to the Spirit*, the Spirit takes control of our lives and leads us to live out God's good will. Self-control is thus not about *trying hard* but about *yielding hard*. Self-control is yielding to God's power to do the things we should and to not do the things we shouldn't.

Self-control is truly impossible in our own strength. Our sin nature will wear us down and get the best of us. Thankfully, as believers we have the power of God within us to live a life not undermined by our inner desires and the corruption of the world. If we truly desire to become like Jesus for the sake of others, we will receive the call and challenge to be self-controlled. As we yield our lives to God's plan, his divine power gives us the strength to say *no* to ungodliness and *yes* to his will. We have the power, through Christ, to control ourselves.

But the fruit of the Spirit is love, joy, peace, forbearance, kindness, goodness, faithfulness, gentleness and self-control. Against such things there is no law. Those who belong to

Christ Jesus have crucified the flesh with its passions and desires. Since we live by the Spirit, let us keep in step with the Spirit (Galatians 5:22–25).

Be very careful, then, how you live—not as unwise but as wise, making the most of every opportunity, because the days are evil. Therefore do not be foolish, but understand what the Lord's will is. Do not get drunk on wine, which leads to debauchery. Instead, be filled with the Spirit (Ephesians 5:15–18).

Better a patient person than a warrior,
    one with self-control than one who takes a city
(Proverbs 16:32).

I can do all this through him who gives me strength (Philippians 4:13).

1. How is surrender to God the first step to self-control?

2. Why are the words "through Christ" important in the battle for self-control?

KEY APPLICATION
WHAT DIFFERENCE THIS MAKES

None of us is exempt from temptation and sliding down a slippery slope to decadence. Given this, growing in the virtue of self-control may just save our lives and the lives of those we love. As Christ takes over more and more territory in our hearts, there is less of our flesh to interfere. The grip of sin is loosened, and God's qualities show in our lives in ever-growing proportions.

Self-control is not only about the discipline to stop doing things that destroy us but also to do the things that build us up. When we develop a healthy discipline to engage in the spiritual practices, we speed up our spiritual growth rate. Furthermore, our connection to others is empowered when we increase in self-control. Disagreements, arguments, outbursts, and misguided emotions are held at bay as we learn to control our tongues. As we yield to the love, grace, and presence of Christ within us, we move toward the victory.

The Bible offers practical instruction on how to grow in self-control. One way is to *flee* from the person, environment, or situation that tempts us to lose control. A second strategy, also defensive in nature, is to *resist*. We can tame our tongues, reduce fights and quarrels, control our selfish desires, and mitigate the negative influences of the world and the devil.

Ultimately, complete self-control in this life is unattainable. Our sin nature, or flesh, will sometimes make us weary and weak. So again, the ultimate solution to gain self-control is God-control. We have access to God's presence and power to guide us and give us strength. As believers, we can use this strength to grow in self-control and live godly lives.

Submit yourselves, then, to God. Resist the devil, and he will flee from you. Come near to God and he will come near to you (James 4:7–8).

Be alert and of sober mind. Your enemy the devil prowls around like a roaring lion looking for someone to devour. Resist him, standing firm in the faith, because you know that the family of believers throughout the world is undergoing the same kind of sufferings (1 Peter 5:8–9).

For this very reason, make every effort to add to your faith goodness; and to goodness, knowledge; and to knowledge, self-control; and to self-control, perseverance; and to perseverance, godliness; and to godliness, mutual affection; and to mutual affection, love. For if you possess these qualities in increasing measure, they will keep you from being ineffective and unproductive in your knowledge of our Lord Jesus Christ (2 Peter 1:5–8).

1. What does "God-control" look like in the lives of believers in Christ?

   _____

   _____

   _____

   _____

2. What encouragement do you have as a believer when the battle for self-control doesn't seem to be going well?

   _____

   _____

   _____

   _____

EVALUATE

As you conclude this personal study, use a scale of 1–6 to rate how strongly you believe the following statements (1 = no belief at all, 6 = complete confidence):

___ I am not addicted to any substances—whether food, caffeine, tobacco, alcohol, or chemical.

___ I do not burst out in anger toward others.

___ I do not have sexual relationships that are contrary to biblical teaching.

___ I control my tongue.

TAKE ACTION

Memorizing Scripture is a valuable discipline for all believers to exercise. Spend a few minutes each day committing this week's key verse to memory.

KEY VERSE: "For the grace of God has appeared that offers salvation to all people. It teaches us to say 'No' to ungodliness and worldly passions, and to live self-controlled, upright and godly lives in this present age, while we wait for the blessed hope—the appearing of the glory of our great God and Savior, Jesus Christ" (Titus 2:11–13).

Recite this week's key idea out loud. As you do, ask yourself, *Does my life reflect this statement?*

> **KEY IDEA:** I have the power through Christ to control myself.

Answer the following questions to help you apply this week's key idea to your own life.

1. How would this virtue express itself in your life?

   _____

   _____

   _____

2. What visible attributes can be found in someone who is self-controlled?

   _____

   _____

   _____

3. What is impeding your ability to display self-control? How can you overcome this obstacle?

   _____

   _____

   _____

4. What step can you take this week to increase your ability to flee from and resist ungodly situations?

_____

_____

_____

_____

_____

_____

Session 5

HOW CAN I MAINTAIN HOPE DURING HARDSHIPS?

My mom had a debilitating fear of flying. For her, traveling by plane wasn't an option when it came to visiting family that lived out of state. But this all changed when our daughter was born. The only way Mom could see her new granddaughter was to fly from where she lived in Cleveland to Dallas. So, she summoned all her courage and made the trip. The hope of seeing her new grandbaby allowed her to overcome her lack of faith in air travel, because she so desperately wanted to see the person at the other end of the journey. Faith offers us the *belief* of eternity. But we *live* by the hope that Jesus is at the other end of our journey.

VIDEO TEACHING NOTES

Welcome to session five of *Be Like Jesus*. Spend a few minutes sharing any insights or questions about last week's personal study. Then start the video and use the following outline to record some of the main points. (The answer key is found at the end of the session.)

- **Key Question**: How do I _____
  with the hardships and struggles of life?

- **Key Idea**: I can _____
  with the hardships of life because of the hope I
  have in Jesus Christ.

- The first cause: believe in the _____
  The second cause: believe in the _____
  _____ making the promise.

- **Key Verse**: "We have this _____
  _____ as an anchor for the
  soul, firm and secure. It enters the inner sanctuary
  behind the curtain, where our forerunner, Jesus,
  has entered on our behalf" (Hebrews 6:19–20).

- **(Key Application #1)**: If you want to increase your
  hope, get to know and _____
  _____ Jesus better.

- **(Key Application #2)**: If you want to increase your
  hope, get to know and trust Jesus' _____.

GETTING STARTED

Begin your discussion by reciting the key verse and key idea together as a group. On your first attempt, use your notes if you need help. On your second attempt, try to state them completely from memory.

KEY VERSE: "We have this hope as an anchor for the soul, firm and secure. It enters the inner sanctuary behind the curtain, where our forerunner, Jesus, has entered on our behalf" (Hebrews 6:19–20).

KEY IDEA: I can cope with the hardships of life because of the hope I have in Jesus Christ.

GROUP DISCUSSION

As a group, discuss your thoughts and feelings about the following declarations. Which statements are easy to declare with certainty? Which are more challenging? Why?

- I think a great deal about heaven and what God is preparing for me as a Christian.
- I am confident that God is working everything out for my good, regardless of the circumstances today.
- My hope in God increases through my daily pursuit to live like Christ.

- My hope for the future is not found in my health or wealth because both are so uncertain, but in God.

Based on your group's dynamics and spiritual maturity, choose two or three questions that will lead to the best discussion about this week's key idea.

1. We are all guilty at times of placing our faith in false hopes. Which one (riches, people, idols, human government) is most alluring to you? Why?

2. In what ways have false hopes let you down in the past?

3. Hope is not an emotion you can make yourself feel through willpower. So what action steps can you take in order to develop a greater sense of hope?

4. What experiences with God have increased your ability to trust him and his promises?

_____

_____

_____

_____

_____

Read Hebrews 11:1–12:3 and choose one or two questions that will lead to the greatest discussion in your group.

1. Faith and hope seem to be the underlying characteristics of all biblical heroes. In what ways do these characteristics work together?

_____

_____

_____

_____

_____

2. Which character's story of faith do you feel exhibited the most hope in God's promises? Why?

_____

_____

_____

_____

3. It is easy to "grow weary and lose heart" in this broken world. What does the writer of this passage encourage you to do in order to combat hopelessness?

_____

_____

_____

_____

_____

_____

CASE STUDY

Use the following case study as a model for a real-life situation where you might put this week's key idea into practice.

> Your cousin Rob has trust issues, which is understandable. His dad (your uncle) ran out on the family just before Rob's twelfth birthday. Friends and coworkers have continually taken advantage of his generosity and kindness. In an honest moment on your back porch, he confesses that he believes in God but does not trust him. He goes on to explain that he desires to trust God but fears that his past has caused him to be irreversibly jaded.

Using the following key applications from this session, discuss what you could say or do to help Rob begin to trust in God's character and his promises.

KEY APPLICATION #1: If you want to increase your hope, get to know and trust Jesus better.

KEY APPLICATION #2: If you want to increase your hope, get to know and trust Jesus' promises.

CLOSING PRAYER

Close your time together with prayer. Share your prayer requests with one another. Ask God to help you put this week's key idea into practice.

FOR NEXT WEEK

Before your next group meeting, be sure to read through the following personal study and complete the exercises.

VIDEO NOTES ANSWER KEY
deal / cope / promise, One / hope / trust / promises

PERSONAL STUDY

Last week you examined the virtue of self-control. Perhaps you were encouraged to tame your tongue or rein in your temper. Before your next group meeting, complete the following study. Then allow the truths of Scripture to fill your soul with hopefulness.

KEY QUESTION
HOW DO I DEAL WITH THE HARDSHIPS AND STRUGGLES OF LIFE?

In the Bible, we find that faith and hope are linked together (see Hebrews 11:1). So, as we look at the virtue of hope, it is also important for us to clearly understand what faith involves. Faith is an acknowledgment that even though we have no idea of what is coming ahead, we trust that God knows. We *believe* that he has the future in his control. We place our hope in him.

Our deep need for hope often leads us to falsely put our hope in unhealthy things. False hope causes us to plan, build, and risk for something that is not likely to happen. The Bible identifies several things in which humans unfortunately place their hope—only to be disappointed in the end—including false hopes in riches, people, human government, and idols, which can be defined as *anything* we place above God.

True hope is only found through trust in God. If faith begins the journey, then hope ends it. Hope is knowing where the road of faith will end—and being confident of where the story concludes. Christian hope is an anchor for our souls. It stabilizes us during difficult seasons because we know this is not how our story ends. It is rooted in our belief and trust in a personal God, his salvation, and eternity. Believing these things in our heart produces a hope that doesn't disappoint.

Hope gives us the ability to endure the hardships and difficulties along the road of faith. We walk on in the hope of where the road leads: to eternity with Jesus.

Now faith is confidence in what we hope for and assurance about what we do not see (Hebrews 11:1).

We have this hope as an anchor for the soul, firm and secure. It enters the inner sanctuary behind the curtain, where our forerunner, Jesus, has entered on our behalf (Hebrews 6:19–20).

"Here now is the man
  who did not make God his stronghold
but trusted in his great wealth
  and grew strong by destroying others! . . .
And I will hope in your name,
  for your name is good (Psalm 52:7, 9).

Command those who are rich in this present world not to be arrogant nor to put their hope in wealth, which is so uncertain, but to put their hope in God, who richly provides us with everything for our enjoyment (1 Timothy 6:17).

1. To what sources of false hope do people often turn?

_____

_____

_____

_____

2. How is hope dependent on faith?

_____

_____

_____

_____

KEY IDEA

I CAN COPE WITH THE HARDSHIPS OF LIFE BECAUSE OF THE HOPE I HAVE IN JESUS CHRIST

To better understand biblical hope, we must first understand what hope is *not*. Hope is not putting our faith in our current circumstances—that they will either improve or at least stay the same. We do not have such a guarantee and thus cannot sustain this type of hope. Such attempts will only lead to colossal disappointments. Hope is only as good as the power and character of the one who guarantees it, which is why *true* hope is only found in God.

Christ offers us something more. He provides what is true and viable—the hope of eternal life. As Christians, we place our hope on the promise of what God has told us will come and the promise that Jesus is on the other side of this life. This promise to believers—past and present—of being with the Lord forever is the foundation of our hope. The grand bonus is that we will be reunited with all those who have gone before us to heaven.

This hope of eternity that God has promised to all believers in Christ enables us to endure life's hardships and endure bumps and bruises along the way. When we hope in God's promises, the effect on our lives is profound. Even if we are going through difficulties, we have the strength to continue. We can hope in the ultimate promise of God: our future resurrection.

We wait in hope for the LORD;
he is our help and our shield.
In him our hearts rejoice,
for we trust in his holy name.
May your unfailing love be with us, LORD,
even as we put our hope in you (Psalm 33:20–22).

In this hope we were saved. But hope that is seen is no hope at all. Who hopes for what they already have? But if we hope for what we do not yet have, we wait for it patiently (Romans 8:24–25).

[I] present to you the word of God in its fullness—the mystery that has been kept hidden for ages and generations, but is now disclosed to the Lord's people. To them God has chosen to make known among the Gentiles the glorious riches of this mystery, which is Christ in you, the hope of glory (Colossians 1:25–27).

1. What promises of God give you hope?

2. How is God's Word a source of true hope?

KEY APPLICATION
WHAT DIFFERENCE THIS MAKES

On a day-to-day basis, we have little choice but to stay focused on our physical world. We have bills that need to be paid, problems that are waiting to be solved, and people who demand our attention. Yet hope of a future where God resides and is in control, coupled with a home in his renovated and expanded garden for eternity, encourages us to keep looking forward and fix our eyes on him, not on the world. For believers in Christ, the best really is yet to come.

Our minds can be our greatest enemy or our strongest ally. How we think is what we will do and what we will become. When we embrace God's hope, it has a powerful effect on our lives. Focusing on hope for today, our future, and into eternity creates a positive, optimistic, "glass half full" mindset. This mindset is not only a different way to live, but it's also the best way to live. In our mean-spirited culture, the person with an attitude of hope and uplifting thoughts will not only be a healthier person but will also draw others to Christ.

For millions of people, the hope of Christ has driven them to survive mind-boggling trials and die peacefully under unspeakable circumstances. The longing to see their Savior fueled their hearts to endure to the end. We can face death with hope, but the even better news is that we don't have to wait until then. We can experience this hope right now! We can jump on the plane of faith, assured in the knowledge of who and what awaits us on the other end.

> *Even youths grow tired and weary,*
> > *and young men stumble and fall;*
> > *but those who hope in the LORD*
> > *will renew their strength.*
> *They will soar on wings like eagles;*
> > *they will run and not grow weary,*
> > *they will walk and not be faint* (Isaiah 40:30–31).

> *Since, then, you have been raised with Christ, set your hearts on things above, where Christ is, seated at the right hand of God. Set your minds on things above, not on earthly things* (Colossians 3:1–2).

> *Therefore, since we are surrounded by such a great cloud of witnesses, let us throw off everything that hinders and the sin that so easily entangles. And let us run with perseverance the race marked out for us, fixing our eyes on Jesus, the pioneer and perfecter of faith. For the joy set before him he endured the cross, scorning its shame, and sat down at the right hand*

of the throne of God. Consider him who endured such opposition from sinners, so that you will not grow weary and lose heart (Hebrews 12:1–3).

1. How can hope in God's promises for the future affect how you walk in faith today?

————————————————————

————————————————————

————————————————————

————————————————————

————————————————————

2. What opportunities of faith today bring hope for the future—no matter what your circumstances?

————————————————————

————————————————————

————————————————————

————————————————————

————————————————————

EVALUATE

As you conclude this personal study, use a scale of 1–6 to rate how strongly you believe the following statements (1 = no belief at all, 6 = complete confidence):

I think a great deal about heaven and what God is preparing for me as a Christian.

___ I am confident that God is working everything out for my good, regardless of the circumstances today.

___ My hope in God increases through my daily pursuit to live like Christ.

___ My hope for the future is not found in my health or wealth because both are so uncertain, but in God.

TAKE ACTION

Memorizing Scripture is a valuable discipline for all believers to exercise. Spend a few minutes each day committing this week's key verse to memory.

KEY VERSE: "We have this hope as an anchor for the soul, firm and secure. It enters the inner sanctuary behind the curtain, where our forerunner, Jesus, has entered on our behalf." (Hebrews 6:19–20)

Recite this week's key idea out loud. As you do, ask yourself, *Does my life reflect this statement?*

KEY IDEA: I can cope with the hardships of life because of the hope I have in Jesus Christ.

Answer the following questions to help you apply this week's key idea to your own life.

1. How would this virtue express itself in your life?

2. What visible attributes can be found in someone who is filled with hope?

3. What is impeding your ability to experience hope? How can you overcome this obstacle?

4. What step can you take this week to increase your belief in the promises of God?

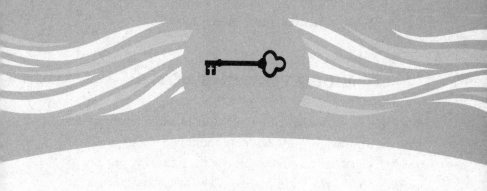

Session 6

HOW CAN I BE PATIENT WITH OTHERS?

Annoying people. Frustrating people. Irritating people. Most of the time, when it comes to our struggles with patience, it's due to other people. We get rude with the ones we love the most, but we can also lose our temper with total strangers. Impatience shows no favoritism. Speaking of which, it's interesting that when we talk about patience, we often refer to *im*patience. We say things like, "You are trying my patience." Or, "My patience is wearing thin." Or, "I'm just about out of patience with you." So much that has to do with our use of the word *patience* refers to our lack of it! We all have stress triggers—buttons that when pushed cause us to lose patience. But if we want to be like Jesus, becoming a more patient person is non-negotiable.

VIDEO TEACHING NOTES

Welcome to session six of *Be Like Jesus*. Spend a few minutes sharing any insights or questions about last week's personal study. Then start the video and use the following outline to record some of the main points. (The answer key is found at the end of the session.)

- **Key Question:** How does God provide the help I need to deal with _____?

- **Key Verse:** "Whoever is _____ has great understanding, but one who is quick-tempered displays folly" (Proverb 14:29).

- **Key Idea:** I am slow to anger and endure patiently under the unavoidable _____ of life.

- "Consider it pure joy, my brothers and sisters, whenever you face trials of many kinds, because you know that the testing of your faith produces _____. Let perseverance finish its work so that you may be mature and complete, not lacking anything" (James 1:2–4).

- (Key Application #1): Trust God's timing, his ways, and his _____.

- (Key Application #2): Don't let unimportant stuff _____ you so much.

- **(Key Application #3)**: Offer the patience today that you would like to _____ tomorrow.

GETTING STARTED

Begin your discussion by reciting the key verse and key idea together as a group. On your first attempt, use your notes if you need help. On your second attempt, try to state them completely from memory.

KEY VERSE: "Whoever is patient has great understanding, but one who is quick-tempered displays folly." (Proverbs 14:29)

KEY IDEA: I am slow to anger and endure patiently under the unavoidable pressures of life.

GROUP DISCUSSION

As a group, discuss your thoughts and feelings about the following declarations. Which statements are easy to declare with certainty? Which are more challenging? Why?

- I do not get angry with God when I have to endure suffering.

- I am known to maintain honesty and integrity when under pressure.
- I always put matters into God's hands when I am under pressure.
- I keep my composure even when people or circumstances irritate me.

Based on your group's dynamics and spiritual maturity, choose two or three questions that will lead to the best discussion about this week's key idea.

1. What current situations test your patience most? Why?

_____

_____

_____

_____

2. What external forces negatively impact your ability to remain patient?

_____

_____

_____

_____

3. How has your relationship with God impacted your ability to be slow to anger in stressful situations?

_____

_____

_____

_____

4. Think of a challenging time in your life that helped you develop perseverance. How did you grow spiritually during that period?

_____

_____

_____

_____

_____

Read 1 Samuel 26:1–25 and choose one or two questions that will lead to the greatest discussion in your group.

1. How did the years David spent waiting to become king prepare him for the responsibility of the throne?

_____

_____

_____

_____

_____

2. In what ways have periods of waiting in the past developed your character?

_____

_____

_____

_____

_____

3. In what ways have you experienced the foolishness of quick-temperedness?

_____

_____

_____

_____

_____

CASE STUDY

Use the following case study as a model for a real-life situation where you might put this week's key idea into practice.

> Kelly has been dreaming about creating her own family since she was a little girl. She was engaged soon after college but felt led by God to call it off. Since then, she has tried numerous ways to find a good husband, but nothing has materialized. Anxiety and fear breed within her as each year passes. She is beginning to believe she will always be alone.

Using the following key applications from this session, discuss what you could say or do to help Kelly.

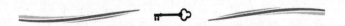

KEY APPLICATION #1: Trust God's timing, his ways, and his outcomes.

KEY APPLICATION #2: Don't let unimportant stuff bother you so much.

KEY APPLICATION #3: Offer the patience today that you would like to receive tomorrow.

CLOSING PRAYER

Close your time together with prayer. Share your prayer requests with one another. Ask God to help you put this week's key idea into practice.

FOR NEXT WEEK

Before your next group meeting, be sure to read through the following personal study and complete the exercises.

VIDEO NOTES ANSWER KEY

stress / patient / pressures / perseverance / outcomes / bother / receive

PERSONAL STUDY

Last week you examined the virtue of hope. Perhaps you were empowered to better handle the hardships of life. Before your next group meeting, complete the following study. Then open your heart and mind to the lessons God wants to teach you through this session.

KEY QUESTION
HOW DOES GOD PROVIDE THE HELP I NEED TO DEAL WITH STRESS?

As many of us fly through life at breakneck speed, levels of patience seem to have dramatically changed—and not for the better. Technology has had a significant impact on our ability to wait. We become frustrated when we have to wait five minutes, whereas just a few years ago we might have had to wait five hours. We no longer want to wait—for anything. The old joke, "Lord, give me patience, and give it to me now!" describes us well.

God provides for our impatient souls in a number of ways. He is long-suffering in dealing with us, which provides an *example* for how we should respond to others. God's Holy Spirit gives us the *strength* and ability to see life through his eyes and by his perspective, which helps us see the bigger picture and impacts the way we handle stress. He also *encourages* us with inspiration and motivating words found in His word to help us wait for his timing.

God models what he desires to see in us. We may struggle to trust him—even after he has proved himself to us repeatedly—but he continues to be gracious and patient with us. If we turn to him, we will find that he will give us the ability to endure, persevere, and be patient.

> *But you, Lord, are a compassionate and gracious God,*
> > *slow to anger, abounding in love and faithfulness*
> (Psalm 86:15).

> *Wait for the LORD;*
> > *be strong and take heart*
> > *and wait for the LORD* (Psalm 27:14).

> *The Lord is not slow in keeping his promise, as some understand slowness. Instead he is patient with you, not wanting anyone to perish, but everyone to come to repentance* (2 Peter 3:9).

1. How does God's patience provide you with the opportunity to learn to trust in him?

2. How does trusting in God in your relationships and circumstances impact how you handle stress?

_____

_____

_____

_____

_____

KEY IDEA
I AM SLOW TO ANGER AND ENDURE PATIENTLY UNDER THE UNAVOIDABLE PRESSURES OF LIFE

Patience falls in the same company as humility, gentleness, and love (see Ephesians 4:2). (Doesn't it make sense that a humble, gentle, loving person would also be patient?) In the Bible, the Greek word *makrothymia* is often translated into English as *patience*, but it also carries the idea of "taking a long time to burn with anger."

Some translations of the Bible use the word *long-suffering* to define patience, which conveys the idea that we will display restraint and be merciful even when we have been wronged. We will not only refuse to defend ourselves but will also turn down any opportunity to offend the other person. We will "suffer long" before we will get upset. Another Greek word that is translated as patience or perseverance is *hypomone*, which literally means "to remain under" the unavoidable pressures of life. We can picture this pressure as a heavy bag we carry on our back.

Certainly, there are self-imposed pressures that we should avoid altogether. But there are some situations that are simply outside of our control. In these unavoidable situations, we might attempt to relieve our pressure by doing the wrong thing—such as by becoming addicted to prescription drugs, getting a divorce, or through seeking revenge. But God encourages us "to remain under the pressure" of this situation because it is the right thing to do—to stay in a relationship and keep working on it, forgive, and move on. God can also give us the resources and the motivation to slowly work toward change in difficult circumstances.

The bottom line is that God wants to offer the *best* solution for everyone inside the circumstances.

> *Whoever is patient has great understanding,*
> *but one who is quick-tempered displays folly*
> (Proverbs 14:29).

> *So do not throw away your confidence; it will be richly rewarded. You need to persevere so that when you have done the will of God, you will receive what he has promised* (Hebrews 10:35–36).

> *My dear brothers and sisters, take note of this: Everyone should be quick to listen, slow to speak and slow to become angry, because human anger does not produce the righteousness that God desires* (James 1:19–20).

> *Never be lacking in zeal, but keep your spiritual fervor, serving the Lord. Be joyful in hope, patient in affliction, faithful in prayer* (Romans 12:11).

1. How would you describe a patient person?

   _____

   _____

   _____

   _____

2. How is patience grown in a person's character?

   _____

   _____

   _____

   _____

   _____

KEY APPLICATION
WHAT DIFFERENCE THIS MAKES

The only way God can help us to grow in patience is to give us circumstances where we must learn to wait on him. Of course, we can quickly get tired of this process and make things happen on our own. But we must recognize at the root of this impatience is mistrust. God wants us to wait, but we doubt whether anyone will act on our behalf, so we choose *not* to wait. In our impatience, we exhibit *pride*.

The truth is that if we really trust God, we will wait on him to act. We will wait on his timing as we commit to serving him as we wait. Also, it is typically true that the faster we want something to occur, the more it means we aren't ready to handle the responsibility. As we mature in Christ, we see more clearly why God's timing is perfect. He knows when we need something. To trust in his provision is far better than placing our selfish demands before him.

Not all our stories are the same, yet we are all called to respond with patience. Waiting on God will always provide the strongest finish and allow us to see things as God sees them. This will, in turn, spill over into our interactions with our neighbors. Showing patience will positively affect our relationships and bring joy to our community.

If we trust God and have a passion to treat others the way he treats us, we will learn more each day how to be slow to anger and tolerate the unavoidable pressures of life. Patience will become a spiritual muscle that grows stronger as we quietly wait for God to answer. Our cultivation of this virtue will be pleasing to God . . . who is always patient with us.

> Trust in the LORD with all your heart
> and lean not on your own understanding;
> in all your ways submit to him,
> and he will make your paths straight
> (Proverbs 3:5–6).

> A person's wisdom yields patience;
> it is to one's glory to overlook an offense
> (Proverbs 19:11).

> The end of a matter is better than its beginning,
> and patience is better than pride.
> Do not be quickly provoked in your spirit,
> for anger resides in the lap of fools
> (Ecclesiastes 7:8–9).

1. How does trusting in God's goodness give you the strength to live patiently?

_____

_____

_____

_____

2. What unavoidable pressures are you facing today where you need to exhibit patience?

_____

_____

_____

_____

EVALUATE

As you conclude this personal study, use a scale of 1–6 to rate how strongly you believe the following statements (1 = no belief at all, 6 = complete confidence):

____ I do not get angry with God when I have to endure suffering.

____ I am known to maintain honesty and integrity when under pressure.

____ I always put matters into God's hands when I am under pressure.

____ I keep my composure even when people or circumstances irritate me.

TAKE ACTION

Memorizing Scripture is a valuable discipline for all believers to exercise. Spend a few minutes each day committing this week's key verse to memory.

KEY VERSE: "Whoever is patient has great under-standing, but one who is quick-tempered displays folly" (Proverbs 14:29).

Recite this week's key idea out loud. As you do, ask yourself, *Does my life reflect this statement?*

KEY IDEA: I am slow to anger and endure patiently under the unavoidable pressures of life.

Answer the following questions to help you apply this week's key idea to your own life.

1. How would this virtue express itself in your life?

_____

_____

_____

_____

2. What visible attributes can be found in someone who is slow to anger?

_____
_____
_____
_____
_____

3. What, if anything, is impeding your ability to respond patiently to life's unexpected pressures? How can you overcome this obstacle?

_____
_____
_____
_____
_____

4. What step can you take this week to grow in the area of patience?

_____
_____
_____
_____
_____

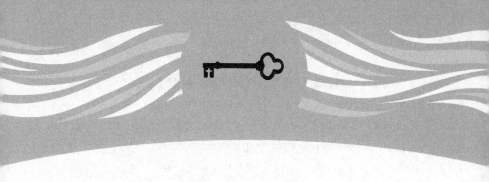

Session 7

WHY SHOULD I BE LOYAL TO OTHERS?

Most people would connect the virtue of faithfulness to the context of a marriage covenant, whether in the positive sense of being faithful or in the negative sense of being unfaithful. Marriage can certainly be one of the best cultural pictures of this virtue. Sadly, however, for too many couples, marriage can become the worst picture of this trait. Some spouses decide faithfulness has a limit and is no longer worth the effort. But there are also those who embrace and embody the biblical definition of faithfulness. These examples of faithfulness are motivated by a deep love and commitment to both Jesus Christ and their spouse. They look to God as the ultimate example of faithfulness, as demonstrated through his love and commitment to us.

VIDEO TEACHING NOTES

Welcome to session seven of *Be Like Jesus*. Spend a few minutes sharing any insights or questions about last week's personal study. Then start the video and use the following outline to record some of the main points. (The answer key is found at the end of the session.)

- **Key Question:** Why is it _____ _____ to be loyal and committed to others?

- **Key Verse:** "Let love and _____ _____ never leave you; bind them around your neck, write them on the tablet of your heart. Then you will win favor and a good name in the sight of God and man" (Proverbs 3:3–4).

- George MacDonald writes, "To be _____ _____ is a greater compliment than to be loved."

- **Key Idea:** I have established a good _____ _____ with God and others based on my loyalty to those relationships.

- **(Key Application #1):** God's faithfulness to us _____ our faithfulness to him and others.

- **(Key Application #2):** God does not call us to be _____ but faithful.

- (Key Application #3): If we _____
  to be faithful, he is faithful and just to forgive us.

GETTING STARTED

Begin your discussion by reciting the key verse and key idea together as a group. On your first attempt, use your notes if you need help. On your second attempt, try to state them completely from memory.

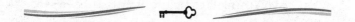

KEY VERSE: "Let love and faithfulness never leave you; bind them around your neck, write them on the tablet of your heart. Then you will win favor and a good name in the sight of God and man" (Proverbs 3:3–4).

KEY IDEA: I have established a good name with God and others based on my loyalty to those relationships.

GROUP DISCUSSION

As a group, discuss your thoughts and feelings about the following declarations. Which statements are easy to declare with certainty? Which are more challenging? Why?

- I take unpopular stands when my faith dictates.
- I discipline my thoughts based on my faith in Jesus Christ.
- I follow God even when it involves suffering.
- I follow through on commitments I have made to God.

Based on your group's dynamics and spiritual maturity, choose two or three questions that will lead to the best discussion about this week's key idea.

1. What do you think is the cause of unfaithfulness toward God or others?

2. Who is an inspirational example of faithfulness to you? Why?

3. In your opinion, what motivates genuine faithfulness?

4. How have you seen suffering test and/or strengthen someone's faithfulness?

_____

_____

_____

_____

_____

Read Ruth 1:1–22 and choose one or two questions that will lead to the greatest discussion in your group.

1. Life for Naomi and Ruth was much different than for us today. Aside from grieving her loss, why would the death of her husband and sons be so devastating for Naomi? Why did she instruct her daughters-in-law to go back to their families?

_____

_____

_____

_____

_____

2. Why was Ruth's decision to stay with her mother-in-law an incredible act of faithfulness?

_____

_____

_____

_____

3. Have you ever witnessed Ruth-like faithfulness in another person? If so, how?

_____

_____

_____

_____

CASE STUDY

Use the following case study as a model for a real-life situation where you might put this week's key idea into practice.

> Deidre had never stepped foot into a church building until she was well into her twenties. Something about church made her feel anxious. She felt like God was upset or disappointed with her. A year ago, she decided to face her fear and get involved at your church. Although she has been consistently involved in church community, she is reluctant to fully devote herself to Christ because she is sure she will mess up and disappoint God in the long run.

Using the following key applications from this session, what could you say or do to help Deidre?

KEY APPLICATION #1: God's faithfulness to us inspires our faithfulness to him and others.

KEY APPLICATION #2: God does not call us to be successful but faithful.

KEY APPLICATION #3: If we fail to be faithful, he is faithful and just to forgive us.

CLOSING PRAYER

Close your time together with prayer. Share your prayer requests with one another. Ask God to help you put this week's key idea into practice.

FOR NEXT WEEK

Before your next group meeting, be sure to read through the following personal study and complete the exercises.

VIDEO NOTES ANSWER KEY

important / faithfulness / trusted / name / inspires / successful / fail

PERSONAL STUDY

Last week you examined the virtue of patience. Perhaps you were challenged to endure more patiently under life's hardships. Before your next group meeting, complete the following study. Take some time to allow the Scripture to enter your mind and prepare your heart to receive anything God wants to teach you through this study.

KEY QUESTION
WHY IS IT IMPORTANT TO BE LOYAL AND COMMITTED TO OTHERS?

God is patient, kind, good, and faithful, among other traits, and we are called to emulate those characteristics. The ultimate example of God's faithfulness is found in the Old Testament. No matter what his people did, how quickly they turned on him, or how long they disobeyed him, God remained vigilant and available to them. In the New Testament, Jesus showed a striking faithfulness both to the Father and to us, accomplishing the redemption of humankind on the cross. He stayed true to who he was and to his calling to bring us back to the Father.

The true path of biblical faithfulness is not an isolated event or events, but a way of life. We must not simply *do* faithful things—we must *be* faithful people. As this happens, it results in faith-filled actions flowing from a faithful heart.

As with all the other virtues, our faithfulness will benefit other people. When we are faithful to them, they will be blessed. And, over time, our faithfulness to others will also have a reciprocal benefit. People will know that we are faithful and can be trusted. But most of all, our faithfulness will please God, who is always loyal and committed to us. Our loyalty and commitment to others will reflect the love that God has shown us.

> Because of the LORD's great love we are not consumed,
> for his compassions never fail.
> They are new every morning;
> great is your faithfulness (Lamentations 3:22–23).

> Let love and faithfulness never leave you;
> bind them around your neck,
> write them on the tablet of your heart.
> Then you will win favor and a good name
> in the sight of God and man (Proverbs 3:3–4).

> Make sure that nobody pays back wrong for wrong, but always strive to do what is good for each other and for everyone else (1 Thessalonians 5:15).

1. How would you describe God's faithfulness to you?

2. What does it mean for faithfulness to be a way of life for the Christian?

_____

_____

_____

_____

KEY IDEA

I HAVE ESTABLISHED A GOOD NAME WITH GOD AND OTHERS BASED ON MY LOYALTY TO THOSE RELATIONSHIPS

Jesus is our model for living out faithfulness in everyday life. In the Bible, we read that "Jesus grew in wisdom and stature, and in favor with God and man" (Luke 2:52). This is a crucial and pivotal sentence in Scripture, because it is the bridge between Jesus' boyhood and the beginning of him fulfilling his divine calling as a young man. The Bible establishes Jesus' birth and presence on the earth through fact and historical reference, and then cuts to the chase, jumping straight to the beginning of Jesus' ministry and path to the cross.

This is one of those key verses where so much is communicated in a few words. Jesus grew in *wisdom*—his knowledge and character were developing beyond his years. He grew in *stature*—he was growing from a healthy boy into a full-grown adult. He grew in *favor with God*—he remained faithful to the Lord throughout boyhood, adolescence, and early manhood. He grew in *favor with man*—his faithfulness to the Lord and increasing wisdom resulted in right relationships and a good name as a man of honor and integrity.

Jesus' example helps us understand that faithfulness and commitment to God results in the best possible life we can live—never exempt from problems or trials, but consistently walking on the right path toward the character and qualities of our Father. Our faithfulness to God and to others brings us favor and establishes a good name for ourselves. A good name established through a life of faithfulness is a boundless gift to pass on to our children.

> He is the Rock, his works are perfect,
> and all his ways are just.
> A faithful God who does no wrong,
> upright and just is he (Deuteronomy 32:4).

> This, then, is how you ought to regard us: as servants of Christ and as those entrusted with the mysteries God has revealed. Now it is required that those who have been given a trust must prove faithful (1 Corinthians 4:1-2).

> Let us hold unswervingly to the hope we profess, for he who promised is faithful. And let us consider how we may spur one another on toward love and good deeds, not giving up meeting together, as some are in the habit of doing, but encouraging one another—and all the more as you see the Day approaching (Hebrews 10:23-25).

1. In what ways will a faithful person be blessed?

_____

_____

_____

_____

2. Why is a good name with God and others so important?

_____

_____

_____

_____

KEY APPLICATION
WHAT DIFFERENCE THIS MAKES

Faithfulness will translate in two ways in our lives. First, we will be faithful to God. No matter who follows or falls away, we remain in God. We won't shrink back when God's commands are not politically correct to obey. As a result, when God looks at us, he will see committed followers. Our motivation for this choice is our love for him and the knowledge that he always does what is best for us. Our own faithfulness is motivated and led by his deep commitment to our lives and eternity. Our commitment to faithfulness leads us to love God more and more.

Second, we will be faithful to others. The people around us will come to know we are loyal, trustworthy, and consistent. They will see that they can count on us, that we will listen intently to them, that we are available, and that we will always answer their call for help. As we do this, we model God's faithfulness through our lives freely given to others. Our commitment to faithfulness leads us to love our neighbors more and more.

Faithfulness must be a priority, regardless of who is watching us. When we are alone or in a crowd, we must be faithful. When we are in good times or bad, we must be faithful. When we are feeling confident or are in doubt, we must be faithful. If we truly want to influence people for Christ, being faithful must not only be a desirable quality but also a *lifestyle*. We all have the opportunity to open our lives to God's will and demonstrate his faithfulness. The results of such faithfulness will be great and beautiful as God works through those who believe.

> The LORD is my strength and my shield;
>   my heart trusts in him, and he helps me.
> My heart leaps for joy,
>   and with my song I praise him (Psalm 28:7).

> The LORD makes firm the steps
>   of the one who delights in him;
> though he may stumble, he will not fall,
>   for the LORD upholds him with his hand. . . .
> Turn from evil and do good;
>   then you will dwell in the land forever.
> For the LORD loves the just
>   and will not forsake his faithful ones
> (Psalm 37:23–24, 27–28).

> Each of you should use whatever gift you have received to serve others, as faithful stewards of God's grace in its various forms. If anyone speaks, they should do so as one who speaks the very words of God. If anyone serves, they should do so with the strength God provides, so that in all things God may be praised through Jesus Christ. To him be the glory and the power for ever and ever. Amen (1 Peter 4:10–11).

1. Who are some of the most faithful people you know? How do they display loyalty and commitment to God and others?

_____

_____

_____

_____

2. How can your example of faithfulness impact your children and others close to you?

_____

_____

_____

_____

EVALUATE

As you conclude this personal study, use a scale of 1–6 to rate how strongly you believe the following statements (1 = no belief at all, 6 = complete confidence):

_____ I take unpopular stands when my faith dictates.
_____ I discipline my thoughts based on my faith in Jesus Christ.
_____ I follow God even when it involves suffering.
_____ I follow through on commitments I have made to God.

TAKE ACTION

Memorizing Scripture is a valuable discipline for all believers to exercise. Spend a few minutes each day committing this week's key verse to memory.

KEY VERSE: "Let love and faithfulness never leave you; bind them around your neck, write them on the tablet of your heart. Then you will win favor and a good name in the sight of God and man" (Proverbs 3:3–4).

Recite this week's key idea out loud. As you do, ask yourself, *Does my life reflect this statement?*

KEY IDEA: I have established a good name with God and others based on my loyalty to those relationships.

Answer the following questions to help you apply this week's key idea to your own life.

1. How could this virtue express itself in your life?

2. What visible attributes can be found in someone who exhibits faithfulness?

_____
_____
_____
_____
_____

3. What is impeding your ability to be faithful to God and others? How can you overcome this obstacle?

_____
_____
_____
_____
_____

4. What action step can you take this week to increase your faithfulness?

_____
_____
_____
_____
_____

Session 8

HOW CAN I BE CONSIDERATE OF OTHERS?

WELCOME

The quality of gentleness appears to be rare in our culture—even among Christians. Yet this virtue is key to our lives, for nothing can kill a family, friendship, neighborhood, or even a church like pride, arrogance, anger, closed ears, and raised voices. God is all about community, and he calls his followers to likewise be about community . . . and demonstrate gentleness. In the New Testament, the word for *gentleness* actually comes from a medical term and is associated with a mild medication. Essentially, we could say a gentle person is one who is easy on our stomachs, while the person without gentleness causes our stomach to double up in knots. God wants us to be healing agents in the lives of those around us.

VIDEO TEACHING NOTES

Welcome to session eight of *Be Like Jesus*. Spend a few minutes sharing any insights or questions about last week's personal study. Then start the video and use the following outline to record some of the main points. (The answer key is found at the end of the session.)

- **Key Idea:** I am thoughtful, considerate, and calm in my _____ with others.

- **Key Verse:** "Let your _____ be evident to all. The Lord is near" (Philippians 4:5).

- **Key Question:** How do I _____ _____ thoughtfulness and consideration?

- "A _____ answer turns away wrath, but a harsh word stirs up anger" (Proverbs 15:1).

- (**Key Application #1**): Be _____.

- (**Key Application #2**): Be _____.

- (**Key Application #3**): Be _____.

GETTING STARTED

Begin your discussion by reciting the key verse and key idea together as a group. On your first attempt, use your notes if you need help. On your second attempt, try to state them completely from memory.

KEY VERSE: "Let your gentleness be evident to all. The Lord is near" (Philippians 4:5).

KEY IDEA: I am thoughtful, considerate, and calm in my dealings with others.

GROUP DISCUSSION

As a group, discuss your thoughts and feelings about the following declarations. Which statements are easy to declare with certainty? Which are more challenging? Why?

- I consider my own shortcomings when faced with the failures of others.
- I am known as a person who is sensitive to the needs of others.
- I am known for not raising my voice.
- I allow people to make mistakes.

Based on your group's dynamics and spiritual maturity, choose two or three questions that will lead to the best discussion about this week's key idea.

1. Why do you think gentleness is so challenging for believers to grasp?

   _____

   _____

   _____

   _____

2. Consider someone in your life who has the ability to be calm and collected in stress-filled moments. How did he or she manage to develop this virtue?

   _____

   _____

   _____

3. Are there certain circumstances in your life that make gentle conduct nearly impossible? How could your relationship with God empower you to alter your reaction to this situation?

   _____

   _____

   _____

4. In what ways can Jesus' life be a guiding example of gentleness for you when you face difficulties?

   _____

   _____

   _____

Read Matthew 7:1–5, 1 Timothy 3:1–4, and James 3:17–18 and choose one or two questions that will lead to the greatest discussion in your group.

1. How does judgment choke your ability to be calm, considerate, and thoughtful?

2. Why do you think the Bible specifically instructs authority figures to be gentle with the people under their care?

3. If judgment leads to anger and quarreling, what does gentleness produce?

CASE STUDY

Use the following case study as a model for a real-life situation where you might put this week's key idea into practice.

Sean has invested incalculable amounts of time and money into the development of his youngest son, Cade. The results have been infuriating. Cade has flunked out of college twice. Sean has used family and business contacts to help Cade find good jobs, but Cade's work ethic is rotten. Consequently, he lost every job Sean set up for him. As a believer, Sean wants to do what is right, but he can hardly hold back the rage he feels toward his son.

Using the following key applications from this session, discuss what you could say or do to help Sean.

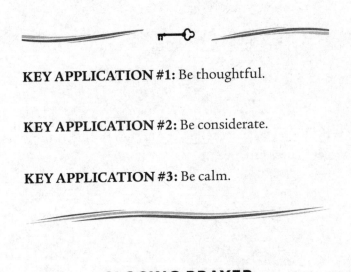

KEY APPLICATION #1: Be thoughtful.

KEY APPLICATION #2: Be considerate.

KEY APPLICATION #3: Be calm.

CLOSING PRAYER

Close your time together with prayer. Share your prayer requests with one another. Ask God to help you put this week's key idea into practice.

FOR NEXT WEEK

Be sure to read through the following personal study and complete the exercises.

VIDEO NOTES ANSWER KEY

dealings / gentleness / demonstrate / gentle / thoughtful / considerate / calm

PERSONAL STUDY

Last week you examined the practice of faithfulness. Perhaps you were challenged to build a trustworthy reputation for yourself. Sometime soon, complete the following study. Take some time to allow the Scripture to enter your mind and open your heart to the lessons that God wants to teach you. Then share what you've learned with someone in your group.

KEY QUESTION
HOW DO I DEMONSTRATE THOUGHTFULNESS AND CONSIDERATION TOWARD OTHERS?

Gentleness is expressed through thoughtfulness and consideration of others. It requires humility, which involves valuing and esteeming others above ourselves. Proud and inconsiderate people want to dominate a room and have their opinions heard. Humble and considerate people desire to make their contributions to a room be about those who are in it. Pride causes people to make assumptions about what others think or feel. Gentleness and humility cause people to empathize and seek to understand what others think and feel.

Throughout the Bible, we read stories that reinforce the idea that gentleness and humility are traits God intends for us to model. Of course, Jesus is our greatest example of someone who displayed gentleness. Jesus' relationship with Peter is a prime example. At the Last Supper, Jesus predicted that Peter would betray him, which came to pass (see John 13:31–38; 18:15–18, 25–27). But later, with a heart of gentleness, Jesus restored Peter and reinstated him to a position of responsibility in the church (see John 21:1–19). Peter isn't the only one Jesus spoke to with gentleness. Jesus invites *all* people to receive his gift of peace and rest.

In Jesus' view, those who exalt themselves and push their own agendas are at the opposite extreme of those who are his followers. In the end, his kingdom will be revealed as contrary to the way that things are in this world. All those who have lived to be exalted will be humbled, while those who have served him and their neighbors in gentleness will be rewarded.

Let your gentleness be evident to all. The Lord is near (Philippians 4:5).

I urge you to live a life worthy of the calling you have received. Be completely humble and gentle; be patient, bearing with one another in love. Make every effort to keep the unity of the Spirit through the bond of peace (Ephesians 4:1–3).

"Come to me, all you who are weary and burdened, and I will give you rest. Take my yoke upon you and learn from me, for I am gentle and humble in heart, and you will find rest for your souls. For my yoke is easy and my burden is light" (Matthew 11:28–30).

1. Why do you think so many people struggle with the virtue of gentleness?

_____

_____

_____

2. Based on what you know of Jesus' example, how would you define *gentleness*?

_____

_____

_____

KEY IDEA
I AM THOUGHTFUL, CONSIDERATE, AND CALM IN MY DEALINGS WITH OTHERS

The words translated as *gentleness* in the New Testament carry the connotations of being thoughtful, considerate, and calming. Gentleness also carries an attitude of strength, much like the power of a tamed animal who chooses to allow its power to be controlled. Gentle people are not weak, but rather strong, secure, and mature. They use their strength to face real giants and challenges in their lives, but choose not to run roughshod over others. This gentleness reflects what Christ wants to see in us as we become gentle for the sake of others.

Our gentleness toward others is most tested when things are not going our way—when we are frustrated, tired, or discouraged. In such situations, we have to choose how to respond. We can decide to lose our temper and lash out in anger, or we can decide to encourage others in Christ. Furthermore, when we face opposition, we need to examine our motives and choose our responses carefully. Our goal is to please God, not seek the praise of people. Often that means being vulnerable, honest, humble, and having an attitude of service toward those who expect a negative response from us. Our gentleness will surprise them and make an impression.

Responding to others in gentleness may cost us something personally in the short-term, but it will mean something greater for the gospel in the long-term. In all things, our goal must be to represent Christ well for the sake of sharing him with others.

> *Do not let any unwholesome talk come out of your mouths, but only what is helpful for building others up according to their needs, that it may benefit those who listen. And do not grieve the Holy Spirit of God, with whom you were sealed for the day of redemption. Get rid of all bitterness, rage and anger, brawling and slander, along with every form of malice. Be kind and compassionate to one another, forgiving each other, just as in Christ God forgave you* (Ephesians 4:29–32).

> *Therefore, as God's chosen people, holy and dearly loved, clothe yourselves with compassion, kindness, humility, gentleness and patience. Bear with each other and forgive one another if any of you has a grievance against someone. Forgive as the Lord forgave you. And over all these virtues put on love, which binds them all together in perfect unity* (Colossians 3:12–14).

Do nothing out of selfish ambition or vain conceit. Rather, in humility value others above yourselves, not looking to your own interests but each of you to the interests of the others. In your relationships with one another, have the same mindset as Christ Jesus (Philippians 2:3–5).

But the wisdom that comes from heaven is first of all pure; then peace-loving, considerate, submissive, full of mercy and good fruit, impartial and sincere (James 3:17).

1. Why is demonstrating thoughtfulness and consideration often a surprising response?

2. What is your motivation for being gentle in your dealings with others?

KEY APPLICATION
WHAT DIFFERENCE THIS MAKES

Gentleness is rooted in our belief in humanity. When we see people the way God sees them, we are compelled to treat them well. Gentle people, according to God's vision, are thoughtful. They take the time to accurately assess a situation and get the whole story before making a response. They do not take anything for granted and think of others first. Over time, they become known for doing little things to encourage people.

Gentle people are also considerate. They do their best to put themselves in the other person's shoes. They are calm, even-tempered, and respond to even stressful situations with positive energy. This attitude and mindset places them in a position of strength when dealing with heated situations and people. Gentle people seek to live in a way that allows them time to breathe and pace themselves. This gives them room to respond in a godly manner.

It can be difficult to know how we are doing in responding with gentleness. Asking others can help. Of course, it will take someone who is secure enough in Christ to tell us the truth in love. But as we learn how to be gentle, little by little we will become more like Christ—and people will be more open to sharing their thoughts with us. Ultimately, with Christ in us, we can be gentle and display the love of Jesus to the world.

Don't have anything to do with foolish and stupid arguments, because you know they produce quarrels. And the Lord's servant must not be quarrelsome but must be kind to everyone, able to teach, not resentful (2 Timothy 2:23–24).

Your beauty should not come from outward adornment, such as elaborate hairstyles and the wearing of gold jewelry or fine clothes. Rather, it should be that of your inner self, the unfading beauty of a gentle and quiet spirit, which is of great worth in God's sight (1 Peter 3:3–4).

Be like-minded, be sympathetic, love one another, be compassionate and humble. Do not repay evil with evil or insult with insult. On the contrary, repay evil with blessing, because to this you were called so that you may inherit a blessing (1 Peter 3:8–9).

1. What does it involve for you to look at life from another person's perspective and put that individual's needs above your own?

2. What preparation do you think a believer needs to make to show thoughtfulness and consideration to others?

EVALUATE

As you conclude this personal study, use a scale of 1–6 to rate how strongly you believe the following statements (1 = no belief at all, 6 = complete confidence):

____ I consider my own shortcomings when faced with the failures of others.
____ I am known as a person who is sensitive to the needs of others.
____ I am known for not raising my voice.
____ I allow people to make mistakes.

TAKE ACTION

Memorizing Scripture is a valuable discipline for all believers to exercise. Spend a few minutes each day committing this week's key verse to memory.

KEY VERSE: "Let your gentleness be evident to all. The Lord is near" (Philippians 4:5).

Recite this week's key idea out loud. As you do, ask yourself, *Does my life reflect this statement?*

KEY IDEA: I am thoughtful, considerate, and calm in my dealings with others.

Answer the following questions to help you apply this week's key idea to your own life.

1. How could this virtue express itself in your life?

_____

_____

_____

_____

2. What visible attributes can be found in someone who is consistently gentle?

3. What is impeding your ability to treat people gently? How can you overcome this obstacle?

4. What action step can you take this week to become a gentler person?

LEADER'S GUIDE

Thank you for your willingness to lead your group through this study! What you have chosen to do is valuable and will make a great difference in the lives of others. The rewards of being a leader are different from those of participating, and we hope that as you lead you will find your own walk with Jesus deepened by this experience.

Be Like Jesus is an eight-session study built around video content and small-group interaction. As the group leader, just think of yourself as the host of a dinner party. Your job is to take care of your guests by managing all the behind-the-scenes details so that when everyone arrives, they can just enjoy time together.

As the group leader, your role is not to answer all the questions or reteach the content—the video and study guide will do most of that work. Your job is to guide the experience and cultivate your small group into a kind of teaching community. This will make it a place for members to process, question, and reflect—not receive more instruction.

Before your first meeting, make sure everyone in the group gets a copy of the study guide. This will keep everyone on the same page and help the process run more smoothly. If some group members are unable to purchase the guide, arrange it so that people can share the resource with other group members. Giving everyone access to all the material will position this study to be as rewarding an experience as possible. Everyone should feel free to write in his or her study guide and bring it to group every week.

SETTING UP THE GROUP

You will need to determine with your small group how long you want to meet each week so that you can plan your time accordingly. Generally, most groups like to meet for either ninety minutes or two hours, so you could use one of the following schedules:

SECTION	90 MINUTES	120 MINUTES
WELCOME (members arrive and get settled)	10 minutes	15 minutes
WATCH (watch the teaching material together and take notes)	15 minutes	15 minutes
DISCUSS (recite the key verse and key idea and discuss the study questions you selected)	40 minutes	60 minutes
CASE STUDY (go through the case study using the key applications for the session)	15 minutes	20 minutes
PRAY (close your time in prayer)	10 minutes	10 minutes

As the group leader, you will want to create an environment that encourages sharing and learning. A church sanctuary or formal classroom may not be as ideal as a living room in this regard, because those locations can feel formal and less intimate. No matter what setting you choose, provide enough comfortable seating for everyone, and, if possible, arrange the seats in a semicircle so everyone can see the video easily. This will make transition between the video and group conversation more efficient and natural.

Try to get to the meeting site early so you can greet participants as they arrive. Simple refreshments create a welcoming atmosphere and can be a wonderful addition to a group study evening. Try to take food and pet allergies into account to make your guests as comfortable as possible. You may also want to consider offering childcare to couples with children who want to attend. Finally, be sure your media technology is working properly. Managing these details up front will make the rest of your group experience flow smoothly and provide a welcoming space to engage the content of *Be Like Jesus*.

STRUCTURING THE GROUP TIME

Once everyone has arrived, it's time to begin the group. Here are some simple tips to make your group time healthy, enjoyable, and effective.

First, begin the meeting with a short prayer and remind the group members to put their phones on silent. This is a way to make sure you can all be present with one another and with God. Next, watch the video and instruct the participants to follow along in their guides and take notes. After the video teaching, have the group recite the key verse and key idea together before moving on to the discussion questions.

Encourage all the group members to participate in the discussion, but make sure they know they don't have to do so. As the discussion progresses, you may want to follow up with comments such as, "Tell me more about that," or, "Why did you answer that way?" This will allow the group participants to deepen their reflections and invite meaningful sharing in a nonthreatening way.

Note that you have been given multiple questions to use in each session, and you do not have to use them all or even follow them in order. Feel free to pick and choose questions based on either the needs of your group or how the conversation is flowing. Also, don't be afraid of silence. Offering a question and allowing up to thirty seconds of silence is okay. It allows people space to think about how they want to respond and also gives them time to do so.

As group leader, you are the boundary keeper for your group. Do not let anyone (yourself included) dominate the group time. Keep an eye out for group members who might be tempted to "attack" folks they disagree with or try to "fix" those having struggles. These kinds of behaviors can derail a group's momentum, so they need to be steered in a different direction. Model active listening and encourage everyone in your group to do the same. This will make your group time a safe space and create a positive community.

CONCLUDING THE GROUP TIME

Each session in *Be Like Jesus* ends with a case study to help the group members process the key concepts and apply them to a real-life situation. At the conclusion of session one, invite the group members to complete the between-sessions personal studies for that week. Explain that you will be providing some time before the video teaching next week for anyone to share insights. (Do this as part of the opening "Welcome" beginning in session two, right before you watch the video.) Let them know sharing is optional.

Thank you again for taking the time to lead your group and helping them to understand what it means to *Be Like Jesus*. You are making a difference in the lives of others and having an impact for the kingdom of God!

What Do I Believe and Why Does It Matter?

What you believe drives everything. The way you behave, the habits you form, the character that defines you at your core—all are driven by what you believe.

It's not enough to believe something as the right answer; you must believe it as a way of life.

The *Think Like Jesus* eight-session video Bible study helps you understand the key beliefs of Christianity that, when embraced in the mind and heart, create true change in your individual life, in the church, and in the world.

Grounded in carefully selected Scripture, *Think Like Jesus* will take you on a journey to become more like Jesus in your beliefs. This revised study, adapted from Part 1 of the *Believe* churchwide study, includes an updated study guide, with new content and questions adapted from the existing *Believe Study Guide* and *Think, Act, Be Like Jesus* by Randy Frazee.

Study Guide
9780310118534

DVD
9780310118558

Sessions Include:

1. Who Is God?
2. Does God Care About Me?
3. How Do I Have a Relationship with God?
4. How Does the Bible Guide My Life?
5. Who Am I in Christ?
6. What is the Purpose of the Church?
7. How Does God Value People?
8. What Is Eternity Going to Be Like?

Available now at your favorite bookstore,
or streaming video on StudyGateway.com.

How Can I Put My Faith into Action?

Understanding what you believe is just the beginning. To become like Jesus, your beliefs need to not only *inform* you but also *transform* you.

It is the practices of reaching up to God and out to others that drive beliefs from your head ... to your heart.

The *Act Like Jesus* eight-session video Bible study teaches you the life-giving spiritual disciplines that will lead you in fulfilling your mission to love God and love your neighbor.

Grounded in carefully selected Scripture, *Act Like Jesus* will take you on a journey to become more like Jesus in your behaviors. This revised study, adapted from Part 2 of the *Believe* churchwide study, includes an updated study guide, with new content and questions adapted from the existing *Believe Study Guide* and *Think, Act, Be Like Jesus* by Randy Frazee.

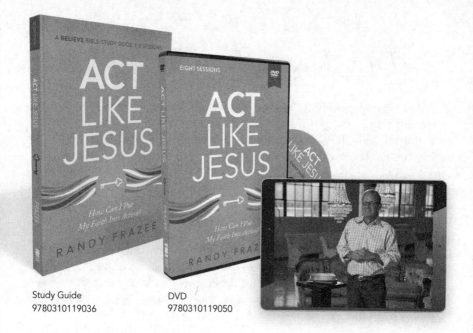

Study Guide
9780310119036

DVD
9780310119050

Sessions Include:

1. How Do I Worship God?
2. Why Do I Need to Pray?
3. How Do I Study the Bible?
4. How Much of My Life Does God Want?
5. How Do I Develop Healthy Relationships?
6. What Spiritual Gifts Has God Given to Me?
7. How Do I Use My Money to Serve God?
8. How Do I Communicate My Faith?

Available now at your favorite bookstore,
or streaming video on StudyGateway.com.